DISARMED
An Exceptional Journey

Ginger T. Manley

Ideas into Books® W E S T V I E W
KINGSTON SPRINGS, TENNESSEE

ii

Ideas into Books®
W E S T V I E W
P.O. Box 605
Kingston Springs, TN 37082
www.publishedbywestview.com

ISBN: 978-1-62880-063-0 Perfect Bound
ISBN 978-1-62880-064-7 Smashwords
ISBN 978-1-62880-065-4 Amazon Kindle

First edition, January 2015

Photo credits: All photographs are from the private collection of the author's family, except as otherwise noted.

The author gratefully acknowledges permission to reprint the epigraph quote from *Storypeople*, which is used with permission of Brian Andreas.

He loved her for almost everything she was,

and she decided that was enough to let him stay for a very long time.

Other books by Ginger Manley

Gotcha Covered: A Legacy of Service and Protection, 2009, Published by Westview. Available in soft cover through Internet retailers and in select book sellers.

Assisted Loving: The Journey through Sexuality and Aging, 2013, Published by Westview. Available through Internet retailers in soft cover and eBook versions.

Proud Flesh, 2015, Ideas into Books® WESTVIEW. Available through Internet retailers in soft cover and eBook versions.

Other publications and information are available at http://www.gingermanley.com.

Ginger Manley can be contacted at:

ginger@gingermanley.com

Contents

Preface

Disarmed: An Exceptional Journey is the story of my nearly fifty-year relationship with my husband, John, an arm amputee, known affectionately by friends and family as Captain Hook, the One Million Dollar Man, the Bionic Man, the One Armed Bandit, Stumpy, and Oh No.

I have never known John when he has had two natural arms. According to a woman I interviewed whose own spouse had been traumatically wounded in combat, I am an AfterWife—a woman who marries her husband after he has lost a part of himself. Supposedly that is an easier role to play than it is for a wife who must adapt to a changed husband after the fact. I don't know—and can't ever know—if that is true. This is simply our story.

John has been reluctant to have the story told. He doesn't want to be perceived as a hero even though he has been heroic in many ways. I have also had some reluctance. I don't always want to plumb the depths required to be plumbed for the telling of such a story and I don't want to be perceived as a Pollyanna, even though there have been pollyanna-ish characteristics to me at times.

We are two very different people who met in an amazingly serendipitous, almost fairy-tale moment. Fairy tales almost never materialize as happy ever after, but somehow we managed to survive, then thrive despite the challenges life presented and today we are happily married just shy of fifty years.

Initially I wrote *Disarmed* to tell the funny stories. So many people have told me about experiences from their times with John and his artificial arm and I wanted all the stories to be on the same bookshelf and for other people to laugh in the same way we laugh about them. While there is nothing humorous about being an amputee, at the same time there have been so many funny things that have happened that could not possibly be known unless someone is an amputee or the spouse or friend of one. Sometimes humor has been our only asset, and as the saying goes, you just can't make this stuff up.

Beyond the humor, that damn artificial arm has a life of its own, making this a relationship in which there are inevitably three entities. Any relationship threesome is a setup for a mess, as we say in the south. One other piece is crucial—John is and always will remain a pilot and a competitive athlete and I am and always will remain a registered nurse. Those innate perspectives inform our interactions with each other.

Like every story, this is not complete. To use a brewery metaphor, in the distillation process much of the story evaporated leaving only the essence—the most highly priced and valuable part. The essence of this story, for both armed and disarmed people, is a marriage takes work on both sides and every day brings a chance to choose to go or stay.

Our experience is only ours—others with similar challenges have had far different endings. We did not always live happily ever after, but we are pretty happy to be where we are today. I hope you will join me in this reminiscence of our journey by thinking about what you need to know in whatever journeys and relationships you have. Follow the wisdom of the poet Rumi who teaches, "Your task is not to seek for love, but merely to seek and find all the barriers within yourself that you have built against it."

Ginger T. Manley

Franklin, Tennessee

Introduction

Just before Christmas 2011 national news reports described a horrifying accident experienced by twenty-three-year-old Lauren Scruggs, a model and celebrity TV host in Dallas. Lauren had exited the right side of a small prop plane in which she was a passenger and got tangled up with the whirring propeller, severing her left hand and causing severe trauma to the left side of her head and shoulder. The networks reported she was recovering from her injuries in Parkland Hospital, noting on the third day after the accident her breathing tube had been removed and she had spoken a few words to her father. Further down in the story, John Nance, an ABC television aviation expert and commentator, was quoted as saying such aircraft accidents as this are very rare.

When I saw this story on the Internet a few mornings after Lauren's accident, I turned to my then-seventy-year-old husband who was seated at his desk across the room from where I had been working on my computer, and I said, "This sounds exactly like the accident you had when *you* were twenty-three years-old." I read him some of the details and he replied, "Yes, that does sound like what happened to me."

It had already been a busy morning for him, answering personal correspondence on his e-mail account and typing up a complicated legal opinion to be sent to the government agency for which he contracts as an independent reviewer. His typing was methodic, clicking one by one the letters on the left side of the keyboard with the unsharpened pencil he clinched in his prosthetic left hand. The fingers of his right hand worked all four ranks of that side of the keyboard with the practiced agility he had acquired more than fifty years earlier. Periodically he stopped typing and adjusted his reading glasses with his good right hand, pushing them up on his nose when the left side of the frames slipped down the side of his head over the space where his left ear used to be.

After getting out of bed that morning he pulled on his underwear and pants using his good hand for guiding the correct holes over his legs. Anchoring the left end of the pants waistband with pressure from the stump of his left lower arm, he closed the latch on the waistband in a lapping movement with the right hand.

In his closet he looked at the choices of which prosthesis to wear that day—the more functional hook or the less functional but more cosmetically appealing artificial hand. He chose the hand, which he attached by first wetting his stump with a bit of tap water and then slipping it into the socket of the hard molded casing that attached to the artificial hand, making sure the sensors inside the device lined up well with two specific skin areas on the upper part of the stump. These connections allow him to think about when to open and close the prosthesis by consciously sending signals from his brain to the nerve endings in his arm, much the same as regularly-armed folks do thousands of times a day without being conscious of the process.

It was to be a casual day—no need for coat and tie—so he ruled out a button-up shirt, choosing a polo instead. Drawing the shirt over his head, he tugged it down on the right hemline with his good hand and then reached across and swiveled the closed hand of the prosthesis, placing the artificial hand just below the left hemline of his shirt. He thought the hand to open, then close, grabbing the fabric edge in the clinch, and then he watched the hand pull that side of the polo shirt down over his waist before thinking the hand open again. He re-swiveled the hand into neutral position and let it rest at his side. In a one-handed motion with the right one, he tugged some of the shirt buttons at the neck through their corresponding holes, deciding the top one would remain unbuttoned. He decided to wear slip-on shoes—Topsiders—that morning because it was an easier choice than to tie shoelaces with an artificial hand.

In the bathroom he placed his toothbrush in the again-swiveled artificial hand and locked the hand in place so it would not slip as he applied toothpaste to the brush with his right hand, then he switched the now-ready toothbrush to the right hand for brushing. In his right ear he inserted his single hearing aid, which helps remedy his creeping deafness significantly but not as well as a second hearing aid would do if he had a left ear in which to put it.

Finished with dressing and toilet duties, he stepped into the kitchen and removed his omega-3 fish oil from the refrigerator. Balancing the bottle against his midsection and the counter top and holding a teaspoon with his artificial hand, he poured his daily spoonful of heart-health, managing to spill a little on his shirt and into the sink. He ate some toast spread with honey; the latter of which I pointed out to him had dropped onto his prosthetic hand unnoticed by him. Seeing the golden droplets, he then proceeded to lick the honey off the prosthesis.

After breakfast he needed to replace the contact lens which he had been wearing in his right eye. For several years he had also tried to wear a left eye contact lens, but because of the nerve damage to the left side of his head and face his left eye waters a lot and it is very hard for him to keep the lens from floating out so he has pretty much given up trying to have bilateral contact-corrected vision. Since it is impossible for him to put in a new contact lens with one hand, he asked for my help to insert it. With that task done, he moved on to our shared office to start his day's work. Looking at the weather forecast, he wondered if he would also be able to get in nine holes of golf or perhaps some tennis on this unseasonably warm winter day. If he were able to do either of these activities later on, he would need to re-arm himself with a differently adapted prosthesis.

This was just the first hour of his day. He has been doing all these things, and many more, for almost fifty years, with grace, dignity, skill, and quite a bit of humor—but he did not mention any of the humor in the personal note of encouragement he typed and sent to Lauren later that morning. He just told her that he had once been where she was, and while it might seem impossible to her at this stage of recovery to believe life could go on, he wanted her to know it could.

"She'll be busy learning how to adjust to all of this now," he told me as he placed the stamp on the letter. "Later on maybe she'll be able to laugh about some of it."

Once Upon a Time...

Growing up on the Atlantic Coast, John was a consummate athlete. He played Little League baseball every year he was eligible and later he was a lifeguard on the Jersey Shore, participating in guard tournaments against other beach contingents and wowing the young ladies with his physique and charm.

John competing in a lifeguard tournament on the Jersey Shore, c. 1959.

In 2000 he was inducted into the Sports Hall of Fame for the Pingry School in New Jersey from which he graduated in 1960. As a part of the induction ceremony several of his classmates spoke, recreating verbal memories of his days as a varsity nine-letterman. In their opinion, he was someone who nearly walked on water relative to any athletic pursuit. He was recruited out of high school to try out for Major League Baseball, an offer which he turned down, as he did the several opportunities which came his way to play collegiate football on scholarships.

He wanted to become a Brother Rat at Virginia Military Institute and eventually to become an officer in the United States armed forces. He first considered the U.S. Marine Corps, but he later changed his mind. At the end of his third class year, he contracted with the United States Air Force to become an officer after graduation. He spent part of the summer between second and first class years participating in Air Force officers' camp at Langley Air Force Base in Virginia, an experience which included training in jungle survival.

He began flying lessons while at VMI and obtained his private pilot license through the Air Force in his first class year. On June 6, 1964 he was commissioned as Second Lieutenant in the United States Air Force and received orders to report in thirty days to Moody Air Force Base, nine miles northeast of Valdosta, Georgia for military flight training. The next day he graduated from VMI, receiving the Air Force Times award and the designation of Distinguished

Military Graduate. With school behind him, he returned to his home in Ocean Grove, New Jersey for one last opportunity to sit in the South End Beach lifeguard chair, and then he left the Jersey Shore in early July.

John at VMI, c. 1963

Driving his brand new green turbo-charged Corvair Monza Spyder coupe south towards Valdosta those hot days of early July, 1964, John's thoughts were probably only on Dean Martin crooning *Everybody loves somebody sometime* and The Drifters ultimate beach song, *Under the boardwalk* wafting from his radio—and on getting behind the controls of a jet airplane.

Moody Air Force Base began in 1941 as Moody Army Airfield, planted in the Lakeland Flatwoods Project of far southeastern Georgia. Moody was originally planned to be a Strategic Air Command base, but soon it became an Air Training Command (ATC), and eventually became the 3550th Pilot Training Wing, reflecting the mission of ATC's new undergraduate pilot training (UPT) schools established in the late 1960's. Among the many pilots who have been students at Moody, President George W. Bush trained there for fifty-three weeks from November 1968 to November 1969. Today Moody AFB is home of the 23d Wing of the Air Combat Command (ACC) with 6100 military and civilian personnel located at it and on the two geographically separated units at Nellis AFB, Nevada, and Davis-Monthan AFB, Arizona.

On the day John arrived at Moody, the Beatles had just completed their successful tour of the United States and returned to Liverpool for the premier of *A Hard Day's Night*. That same day, Tony Lema, one of the most popular professional golfers of his era and winner of multiple PGA titles, won his only major golf title, the 1964 British Open at the Old Course at St. Andrews by five strokes over Jack Nicklaus. Two years later Lema and his wife would die at age 34 in an aircraft accident when the twin-engine Beechcraft Bonanza in which they were passengers ran out of fuel on an approach and crashed in a water hazard on the seventh green of the Lansing (MI) Country Club.

As John settled into military life, the Republican National Convention took place in the Cow Palace in San Francisco beginning on July 13, 1964 and resulting in the nomination of Barry Goldwater who became the face of conservatism when he was chosen to run against sitting President Lyndon B. Johnson. Johnson had just signed the Civil Rights Act, passed by Congress in homage to JFK's legacy and the Vietnam conflict was about to heat up.

The young lieutenant moved into a two bedroom apartment in the Bachelor Officer Quarters, sharing space with another unmarried second lieutenant pilot. For the next three months, they attended classes where they learned intricacies of flying jet aircraft and technical skills like ejection procedures and parachute jumping necessary to be successful pilots in the Vietnam conflict. With the basics under their hats, these young Moody pilots began flying T-37's at the basic level and then moved to supersonic aircraft— the T-38's, which replaced the subsonic T-33's as the advanced-level trainer plane— while they awaited orders for their next assignment. By September 1965, more than a year into flight training, John was ready to be sent to Vietnam or wherever his service might be needed.

The primary airplane used for pilot training by the Air Force through the 1950's was the propeller-driven, single-engine Beechcraft T-34A Mentor. T-34's were replaced in many UPT programs by Cessna T-37 jet trainers in the late 1950's. During the changeover to T-37's, many T-34A's were turned over to USAF Aero Clubs for use by non-pilot airmen who wished to learn flying. Air force pilots who already were licensed could borrow these planes for personal use and also could instruct other non-pilots in flying the T-34's.

John piloting a U.S. Air Force T-33 jet, Moody Air Force Base, c. 1965

On Saturday September 18, 1965, John was instructing from the rear seat of a T-34A, as an Aero Club airman in the pilot's seat took off from Moody to fly the short distance to Valdosta Municipal Airport, where they intended for John to de-plane and pick up another plane, then to fly it back to Moody. Nobody could say exactly what happened but somehow on that gorgeous Saturday afternoon in Georgia, he stepped out of the T-34A and was hit directly by the rotating propeller. Witnesses later told him when they reached him he was standing beside the plane trying to walk and had to be restrained by three people in order for them to render emergency care.

A twelve-inch gash was opened down the left side of his head directly above his ear and continuing to below his chin, severing the ear above the lobe and tearing through his skull. Part of his brain spilled out along with the hemorrhage and he soon lost consciousness. More blood poured from the gaping wound in his left shoulder, which nearly cut off the arm at that juncture. His left hand was almost severed about four inches above the wrist, remaining attached to the arm by a tag of skin.

Emergency personnel got him to the local hospital and stabilized him, placing a tracheotomy tube in his neck to allow him to breathe with assistance even though he could not speak aloud while the tube remained there. Surgeons did basic trauma procedures to close the head and shoulder wounds. The dangling hand was deemed unusable and was completely removed. His stump was bandaged and elevated with a sling-like device to try to keep swelling under control and he was placed in a private room. The nearby Moody Air Force Base, where he was assigned, sent round-the-clock shifts of their registered nurses to attend to the wounded pilot while he was in the community hospital.

By the third day he had his tracheotomy—the breathing tube—covered and he was transferred by ambulance from the county hospital to the base hospital at Moody. The story goes that when he regained consciousness after the accident and noticed the bandages over his missing limb and covering his head wounds, he began to grieve his loss, first in silence and then audibly once he could speak again. At about the same time, a buddy phoned him in his hospital room to commiserate, and hearing John's lamentations for his lost limb, the friend pointed out it could have been a lot worse. "You could have lost your pecker," his friend observed.

He was kept at Moody for a few more days then put on a medical transport plane loaded with other wounded service personnel from around the country. A Moody nurse accompanied him on the six-hour flight to Wilford Hall Hospital at Lackland Air Force Base in San Antonio, where America's combat casualties from Vietnam were being sent for rehabilitation. Air Force orthopedic surgeons, neurosurgeons, neurologists, and psychiatrists at Wilford Hall evaluated him. Based on their findings they told him he could expect about a year of inpatient rehabilitation. In private they told his family to prepare for the worst because with injuries like his, they did not know how far to expect his recovery to go.

His mother promptly sold his guitar and his car, thinking a man with one hand and an open traumatic brain injury could never strum chords or maybe even drive again.

Rehab consisted of grueling physical therapy several times a day to regain strength and mobility in the affected limb, psychotherapy to deal with the emotional effects of the trauma, speech therapy to re-learn words that had gone missing along with the part of his brain that fell out, and occupational therapy to equip him to live and thrive as an amputee in a world designed for two-handed folks.

The left side of the brain is responsible for language functions like grammar, vocabulary, and literal meaning, especially in right-handed individuals such as John. While still in Wilford Hall Hospital, he began writing thank-you notes to people who visited and called. He could recall the words "the" and "and" and other simple first-grade vocabulary, but the function connected to spelling of these words was still somewhere with the part of his brain left behind in Georgia. Despite the deficit, he worked diligently and much of his vocabulary, if not his memory, was almost completely recovered at the time he left the hospital.

As a part of vocational therapy, he considered other possible careers and thought he might like to become an attorney. With almost no study time or preparation under his belt, he decided to take the Law School Admission Test (LSAT), a grueling exam taken usually by college seniors who have rigorously studied and practiced before they enter the testing facility. John told the LSAT administrators to forward his test scores to Harvard, Duke, University of Virginia, University of Chicago, and Washington and Lee schools of law. Almost by return mail he was turned down for admission to all of these prestigious institutions, which had probably never seen an admission application accompanied by LSAT scores in the lowest tenth percentile.

About six weeks after the accident, once the swelling was at a minimum and he had some range of motion in his left arm stump, he was fitted with his first prosthesis, a rudimentary hook, and he took his first leave to attend the wedding of his best friend and fellow flight school roommate. He left Wilford Hall for good four months after the accident, determined to make his way in a world where he had no job and no job training, except to be a pilot.

The occupational therapy he received allowed him to care for himself in an almost independent manner, and he moved back to Valdosta and rented an apartment. Six months after the accident, while wearing his hook, he requalified in the T-34A, the same plane that he was flying at the time of his accident. The Air Force did not have any flight jobs for one-armed pilots, however, and at age twenty-four on March 1, 1966, he was medically retired at the rank of First Lieutenant. Remaining interested in law, he opened a private detective agency, investigating wayward husbands for their wives or girlfriends or trying to locate missing money from someone's estate, but there did not seem to be much of a future in this career for him and he closed the business.

On his behalf his father's friend in Chicago made connections with Cartan Travel Agency, and John was hired as a tour manager, responsible for keeping well-heeled mostly female clients happy by accompanying them as they rode trains across Canada or the United States and later as they cruised on the *Lurline*, a Matson Lines ship traveling from Los Angeles to San Francisco and then on around the Hawaiian Islands before completing the voyage back to the mainland.

He took to this work with great enthusiasm, befitting a handsome young man who has an unlimited expense account and first class accommodations in some of the most beautiful locations in the world. Hardly missing a beat, he picked up his athletic skills, competing in trap shoots off the ship and excelling as usual in this sporting competition to the delight of his new found lady friends.

John shooting off the stern of the Lurline, c 1966.

In the summer of 1967 he was promoted to overseas tour manager, and he flew to Europe to begin the first of these scheduled three-week excursions, with the first one set to embark from Lucerne, Switzerland, on July 3. He arrived a week or so early to travel on his own, and the story goes that he met a lovely young woman, a native of Germany, who invited him to her home for the evening. On arrival he greeted her friendly Dachshund, Günter. He and the young lady succumbed to each other's romantic charms and in the passion of the moment his ear became unattached and fell onto the floor. As he was getting himself rearranged again after this tryst, trying discreetly to locate his missing part, he saw Günter happily gnawing on his newly retrieved chew toy.

I grew up in East Tennessee in the heart of southern Appalachia, though I did not really get it that I was Appalachian until quite a while after I was an adult. To me, Appalachians were the destitute people from coal mines and mountain hamlets to whom my Sunday School classes sent pennies and baskets during the winter months. My people had lived in these parts since the early 1800's, homesteading on land taken from the Cherokee by the then new state of Tennessee. My ancestors eventually surrendered that land to the bank when the note was called due just as the Great Depression settled over the world. There was work to be had in the ALCOA plants nearby and at one time or another all of my family worked there. We always had food on the table and clothes on our backs and we knew if we worked hard enough and long enough, we would make it.

There were no Interstate highways in Tennessee in the 40's and 50's as I was maturing, and my vision was limited to the two-lane highways running about 200 miles west over the Cumberland Plateau, east over the Smoky Mountains, and south into Atlanta. I don't recall we ever traveled the northern compass route. I thought I'd like to be a movie star or a nurse. The nurse part won out as I tossed around my chances of becoming self-sufficient after high school. In September 1962 I proudly packed all my newly homemade clothes into the two brand new blue hard-side Samsonite suitcases I received for graduation and headed west to Nashville, where four years later I received a bachelor's degree in nursing.

I missed the so-called Summer of Love taking place in San Francisco in 1967 and remembered later on by those who were there for the free love and free pot that signaled the start of the Sexual Revolution. Twenty-two years old and traveling alone, I fled the United States that spring on the rebound from a failed relationship with a naval aviator, my second broken heart in five years. A year out of college, I had spent the previous eight months working the graveyard shift in the medical and surgical intensive care units at Parkland Hospital in Dallas, where I dealt with more gore and human tragedy than I ever wanted to encounter again. My two roommates had recently married men they met only a few months earlier, and I was terrified something like that might happen to me. I was emotionally armed and dangerous and was determined to avoid American men, especially pilots.

More than ready to have some fun before settling down in what I expected to be a pretty routine adult life, I sold my car and withdrew my meager savings to finance the trip. I sailed from New York Harbor on the *SS United States* on Tuesday April 18 wearing a high-end camel wool suit trimmed in fur—a way-out-of-my class fashion statement that I had bought at a fancy Dallas store for 70% off. It seemed a little out of place in my shipboard space, a four person steerage-level room with two metal bunks and not much more. Despite the apparent social dichotomy I managed to

party my way across the Atlantic with newfound friends from all classes of passengers and when I disembarked at Bremerhaven five nights later, I headed for Heidelberg, where a friend from high school had a job as a civilian working on the U.S. military base there.

Ginger embarks on SS United States from New York City.

I expected to easily get a job as a civilian nurse working on the base, but my timing was exceptionally bad—Charles deGaulle had just booted all NATO troops out of France, and Germany was overrun with American nurses, both officers and civilians. After exploring all my options, I re-packed my uniforms, caps, shoes, and white hose in one piece of luggage and shipped them back to the states. Then I placed one call to a Dallas travel agent and ordered a twenty-one day Eurail pass and another call to a favorite uncle back home and asked him to wire me $300 as a loan. With nothing but Frommer's *Europe on 5 Dollars a Day* book as a guide, I began to travel through Europe and Scandinavia, knowing this would be for me a once in a lifetime opportunity to be a free spirit.

Three months later, I had visited Germany, Belgium, the Netherlands, Luxembourg, Denmark, Norway, Sweden, Majorca (where I saw my first bullfight), some of France, and most of Austria and Switzerland, staying in dollar-a-night hostels or *pensions* and for awhile bunking illegally with my girlfriend in her apartment in the Bachelor Officer Quarters in Heidelberg. To further make ends meet, my dinner was often taken in community kitchens in the various locales. While I could speak a little French, that language did not do me much good in most of the countries, but I adapted, learning enough rudimentary words to survive. When my twenty-one-day Eurail pass expired before I was scheduled to leave Europe, I forged the date on it and continued to ride in first class passenger cars, intending to finish my illegal rides on July 13 when I would fly back to the U.S, from Rome.

In Innsbruck on July 1 I met a group of Austrians who were leading some children on a hike high in the mountains and they asked me to join them. Looking out from one of the peaks where we stopped to picnic, I listened intently for Maria Von Trapp to begin warbling, "The hills are alive with the sound of music." That night I joined a smaller group of the same Austrians who took me with them to a local cafe where we sang and ate until late in the evening.

The next morning I hauled my blue suitcase aboard a first class train car scheduled to travel from Innsbruck to Zurich, a ride of a few hours which would put me in that Swiss city early enough to find my usual dollar-a-night accommodation. When the train was halted by a landslide in the Austrian border town of Feldkirch, I did not feel any real concern at first, but as the hours wore on and we were not moving closer to Zurich, I began to wonder if there would be any decent *pension* rooms still available once we arrived. For the next several hours as we waited for the tracks to be cleared, an annoying American man offered to buy me soft drinks and snacks from the food kiosk that serviced the village. Even though I had precious little disposable cash, I turned him down and scurried to find European travelers with whom to pass the time.

After the train re-embarked I found myself seated in the first-class cabin across the aisle from the persistent American. He introduced himself as John and offered to buy me a drink from the cart that was being rolled down the aisle between seats, and since by then I was really thirsty, I begrudgingly accepted his gesture. When the train finally arrived in Zurich that evening, I checked with visitor assistance and found there were no rooms in my class still available. John heard my laments and offered to get me a room in his hotel, an offer I again reluctantly accepted knowing that one night's fare at his hotel was the equivalent of seven nights in my preferred lodgings.

I was hungry and when he invited me to join him for some wine and cheese, I accepted, now resigned to one evening spent with an American man. By the end of the meal, I was surprised to be feeling some actual attraction towards his quick wit and his handsome looks, and honestly, also towards his better accommodation and dining options. During dinner I first noticed his artificial hand and was impressed by the way he used it almost in the same way as one would use a regular hand when cutting meat or picking up a fork.

We talked about a number of things, including that I was running short on money in the run up to my expected leaving from Rome. He offered to loan me $50, enough to get me in and out of Italy, which I agreed to pay back to him on September 16, a Saturday two months hence when he planned to be back in Chicago. We decided to meet the next night in Lucerne where he was to pick up his first European Cartan tour group and I could pick up my money.

I slept late the next morning and when I checked out the desk clerk asked me if I planned to see Mr. Manley again, since he had failed to pay all of his bill when he checked out from his room earlier. I told her I would be seeing him that night and would pass on her message. In Lucerne I got my usual room, this time in the Women's Alcohol Free Hotel, somewhat equivalent to the YWCA hotel rooms of that time, a drab but clean several-floors-walkup facility with a bathroom down the hall.

John was booked in the second floor Presidential Suite at the Grand National Hotel with a balcony overlooking Lake Lucerne. I met him in the lobby for a drink. He had my money and I signed the agreement to pay him back in full in September. I also told him he needed to even things up with the hotel in Zurich and he said he would do so when he returned there in a few weeks to prepare to meet another tour group. That night, he took me to dinner at a Queen Victoria-era hotel and restaurant overlooking Lucerne and by the next night, July 4, I made up my mind to marry him although I did not tell him of my decision.

The Swiss part of his tour meandered from Lucerne to Lausanne, then to Zermatt and finally to St. Moritz. I moved in with him in Lausanne—he did not resist—and stayed with his tour through St. Moritz, before heading to Rome. At the end of our two-week pre-marriage honeymoon, we were pregnant, very much in lust, and I was planning our wedding, although we had never talked of marriage at that time. I already had my ticket for return to the U.S., leaving from Rome the middle of July, which agenda I kept. Unknown to me at that time, I was embarking on a lifetime journey with this one-armed man. While my initial attraction to him was undoubtedly a youthful mixture of lust and limmerance, I was also curious. *I've never been with an amputee,* I thought. I had never been with very many non-amputees either, but his wearing a prosthesis was somehow disarming to me.

There was no text messaging or e-mails then, but in late July when I started to receive daily telegrams from John sent to my home in Tennessee from somewhere in the Alps telling me how much he missed me, I was pretty sure this was not just a fling. He quit his tour manager job a month later and returned to Chicago, telegraphing me to meet him at the O'Hare airport. I flew there unsure if we would even recognize one another after our whirlwind fling a month earlier, but we did. Without knowing he was a father-to-be, he proposed marriage and I eagerly accepted, countering his suggestion that we wait about six months for the wedding date with my own declaration that maternity wedding dresses are not easy to come by and sooner-rather-than-later would suit me better.

September 16, 1967, two months after we met and the date the loan was due, he and I gathered with our families in the church of my childhood and promised to love one another forever through better and worse, richer and poorer, in sickness and in health, til death did us part. It was two years almost to the day since his accident. His family were elated that he was marrying, thinking his prospects after such an accident were slim, and they were especially thrilled to have him marrying a registered nurse, someone they felt sure could continue to care for him should the need arise.

My family was very worried about the kind of marriage I might be getting into. On our wedding day, I knew virtually nothing about this man, except he had one normal hand—the right one—and one artificial hand—the left one. And he was a displaced pilot trying to find his way in a world where he could no longer fly airplanes for a living.

Leaving our wedding reception we traveled by commercial plane to our new home in Chicago. He took me to dinner the next night at Cafe La Tour, a French restaurant, now long-closed, which was atop the Four-Hundred East Randolph building. He had been living in an apartment in that building with his until-recently-also-single father, and the two men had acquired quite a reputation for their social prowess in both La Tour and in other settings in the Windy City. When his dad re-married in June, rumors of a quake spread throughout the singles community, or so I was told. The maitre d' and other servers at La Tour were delighted to see John, but they expressed their astonishment that he was now accompanied by a wife, since a few months earlier none had been on the horizon.

I was very impressed to be dining in such a beautiful place with a glorious view of downtown. On the menu was a Moselle wine we had enjoyed in Switzerland and it was fun to toast our marriage with a glass of Zeller Schwarze Katz. When my new husband ordered *Escargots Bourguignonne* for $.95 extra as an appetizer for both of us, I tried very hard to appear the sophisticate that he seemed to be, and to my amazement, I enjoyed them.

He rented a four-hundred square-foot furnished apartment for us on Chicago's near north side. We settled into routines of his commuting by train downtown to the flagship Marshall Field's department store, where he had worked part-time as a store detective during breaks between tours, and me taking the bus to work as a registered nurse at a nearby hospital. It was in that tiny flat that I first learned the details of his accident of which he had little actual recall. From stories told me by his mother and his father, it was clear that in their eyes he was a special son, destined for athletic or military distinction, and they were grief-stricken to see him permanently handicapped.

Despite many opportunities to do so while we were together in Europe, I had never really noticed the angry red scar running the length of the side of his head, nor the fact that he could only lift the right side of his mouth when he smiled, or that his left eye drooped, nor had I really paid any attention to his not having a full left ear. I did not see any of these distinctive marks until I saw them in our wedding pictures. Remarking to a college friend about the ear shortly after we were married, I heard her say in response, "All you really need to nuzzle is the ear lobe anyway, and he has that part remaining."

It was in that little apartment where I first saw John paint his prosthetic ear, attempting to render it a color that would match his own skin tone. I was in for another shocker when I discovered his favorite thing to do on Sunday afternoons was to watch the televised bullfights that beamed north from Tijuana to the U.S., an entertainment he had learned to appreciate from his father. At about eight weeks into the marriage I remember looking at him one Sunday sitting on the couch of our tiny apartment, completely engrossed in the Spanish language broadcasts.

What have I done? I thought. I'm pregnant; I've married an amputee who eats snails, who is a military pilot with no hope of returning to the cockpit; someone who wears a painted ear, and now I find he is an aficionado of bullfights.

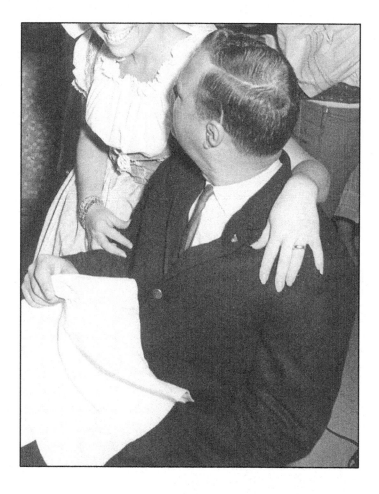

John on one of his tours, with an admirer. Note ear in place.

That damn artificial arm

Writing in *National Geographic* ("The common hand" May, 2012), Carl Zimmer says, "The hand is where the mind meets the world. We humans use our hands to build fires and sew quilts, to steer airplanes, to write, dig, remove tumors, pull a rabbit out of a hat... without hands, all the grand ideas we concoct would come to nothing but a very long to-do list."

A hand and forearm are made of muscles, flesh, bones (lots of them), nerves, ligaments, and blood vessels, all working together to perform fine movements or grand ones and weighing no more than about three pounds each. Other species—orangutans, bats, dolphins, cats, frogs, and even elephants—have hands that have adapted through evolution to whatever action is needed, writes Zimmer. He quotes Charles Darwin, who was intrigued by the hands of all the species he observed, "What can be more curious than that the hand (of all these animals) should all be constructed on the same pattern?"

Popular culture has long been fascinated with amputees. In literature and movies, amputees often are portrayed as having traits of both good and evil, which are frequently in conflict within the same individual or which are crucial to the tension between the character and his nemesis. Sometimes, especially in science fiction portrayals, the altered person receives special strengths when a new body part is attached, as happened with Luke and Anakin Skywalker (later Darth Vader) as well as several other characters in the *Star Wars* episodes.

In the 1970's TV series, *The Six Million Dollar Man*, the protagonist, Steven Austin, who looks and talks like an ordinary person, is actually a bionic man created in a laboratory which makes advanced prostheses. As such he is capable of feats beyond those of ordinary humans. That program was so successful that, like in the Garden of Eden, a female counterpart, *The Bionic Woman* series, was spawned a year or so later.

Probably the best-known literary amputee is the *Peter Pan* character, Captain Hook, a dapper pirate who wears a primitive-styled hook prosthesis. Relative to this story, analysts sometimes say the hook represents its wearer's lost humanity and his evil character.

In the 1996 slapstick comedy, *Kingpin*, Roy Munson, a bowling prodigy who wears a prosthetic hook disguised as an artificial hand, loses in the final round of a $1 million bowling tournament in Las Vegas, but in the end, he gets the girl plus a $500,000 endorsement deal from a condom company, for which he is nicknamed "Rubber Man."

Occasionally the entire plot revolves around a person's artificial limb, as in Currie Alexander Powers' short story, the tragic-comedic *Stick a Fork in Me*. Wendy, a woman whose arm has been amputated in an auto accident when her boyfriend is driving drunk, slips and falls in the aisle of a Target store, dislodging all manner of house ware projectiles, including a fork that embeds in her prosthesis. Wendy lifts a pair of pliers, goes to the restroom and pulls out the fork but resigns herself to the fact that the relationship with said boyfriend is cooked. Powers' story includes a brief sex scene involving the prosthesis, a rare depiction for mainstream literature.

Even animals are becoming fodder for amputee fix-up tales. The story of Midnite, a miniature four-year-old horse born in Texas with only three legs, became a You Tube sensation a few years ago. Midnite was rescued by sheriff's deputies from owners who who could not properly care for him. The deputies took the little horse to Ranch Hand Rescue, a non-profit sanctuary near Dallas. Soon afterwards, the owners of Prosthetic Care, a Fort Worth company specializing in human prosthetics, heard about Midnite and designed and donated a $14,000 artificial limb for him. Within moments of the device being fitted and adjusted to his leg, the tiny horse, which had never run nor hardly ever laid down, since getting up was such a chore, started trotting then galloping with great abandon in his corral. Midnite's courage and desire to be like all the other horses resonates with almost all of humanity.

March 2011

It is 7:30 AM and John and I have gotten up early to join Horace E. Watson, M.D., the head of prosthetics at the Nashville Veterans' Administration Hospital and a Professor of Orthopedics at Vanderbilt University Medical Center, who is engaged in his annual grand rounds presentation entitled "Upper Extremity Amputation Surgery and Prosthetics." Standing behind the podium in a conference room in one of the towers on the Medical Center campus, the distinguished-looking professor, garbed in his starched white lab coat, tells the fifteen or so orthopedics residents in attendance that ten to fifteen percent of all limb amputations are those to upper limbs, a result of trauma, tumors, or vascular disease.

The surgical residents, all male, most wearing blue scrubs, the oldest in his late twenties, listen respectfully to this experienced clinician. At this early morning hour, however, after many of them have been on call the previous night and several are on their way to perform surgery immediately after the mandatory class, it is not uncommon to see them start to drift off.

Dr. Watson describes the seven different levels of upper extremity amputation: partial hand, wrist disarticulation, transradial, elbow disarticulation, transhumeral, shoulder disarticulation, and scapulothoracic. As his Power Point presentation continues through each of these levels, complete with the concomitant prosthetic devices for each one, the residents begin to get restless. Several of them start scrolling through messages on their smart phones, seeming to not hear their professor's words as they manage the complexities of their own lives.

The Power Points show the prosthetic options for single and double disarticulation—the passive, the cable operated, and the myoelectric controlled hand. Using actual patient photographs, Dr. Watson illustrates onscreen the biomechanics of each of these devices. Being careful to relay the need for appropriate medical terminology, Dr. Watson tells the residents that when discussing any specifics of amputation care with a patient, the physician should always refer to the remaining part of the hand, arm, or shoulder as a disarticulated limb and never as a stump.

About forty-five minutes into his presentation, Dr. Watson pauses and introduces the guest speaker to the residents. "Through my work at the VA I've known John Manley for more than thirty years. During that time he's impressed me as a man who doesn't give up. He is an avid golfer and tennis player; a pilot; a lawyer and judge; a father and husband. I've invited John to be here to discuss the daily life of a person with a transradial disarticulation who has vast experience wearing the types of prosthetic devices that I've just been discussing."

Sleep-deprived eyes focus politely on the six-foot tall, balding but still handsome man wearing a sport coat and tie, who steps to the lectern. As he shakes Dr. Watson's outstretched right hand and smiles his greeting, his face seems slightly asymmetrical. He bends his left arm and places his right hand on the artificial hand which extends from the hem of his left jacket sleeve, the bent fingers curled inward towards the floor. With a swift motion, he twists the prosthetic hand ninety degrees to the left with his right hand, places his left elbow on the podium, and clears his throat. Then, with the index finger of his right hand pointing towards the unmoving left hand, he looks deeply into the faces of the young doctors and asks, "How would your life be different if you went to work today and got your hand and part of your arm and your ear chopped off?"

Most all the residents put down their palm-held devices and button their attention on him.

"That's what happened to me just before my twenty-fourth birthday. I didn't want my normal life disrupted so I've always used whatever prosthetic device will allow me to continue to function as if I were never an amputee. If I want to go hunting I put on my rifle-adapted hook. If I want to play golf, I put on my golf-adapted hook. If I want to ski, I put on my ski-pole adapted hand. If I want to carve a turkey I put on my turkey-carving hook. If I want to conduct a trial or lecture to medical residents, I wear my myoelectric hand. If I'm negotiating a labor contract with a particularly stubborn union steward, I put on my hook with the triple strength bands. And that's what you need to know to take care of folks who lose a limb. All of us just want as much as possible to keep on doing what we've always enjoyed doing."

John pauses and makes eye contact one at a time with as many of the young physicians as he can, then with a sheepish look he glances sideways at Dr. Watson and continues.

"And one other thing. I think all of us amps are just fine with you calling it a stump."

John carving a turkey c. 1982

ॐ

Almost all of the amp stories about John begin with "that damn artificial arm of his," like the story that was told recently at the funeral of one of his best friends, Bill S. While most funerals are the occasion for praising the departed, in this instance I think Bill would pardon the little remembrance of John that was also told.

Bill and John met when they were in their thirties and immediately began to play tennis, sometimes in temperatures above 100 degrees and sometimes when there was six inches of snow to shovel off the court before play could start, and in all degrees of comfort in between. Both men were super athletes and they began to compete as a team against teams from other clubs.

Bill had seen the effect on opposing players when John arrived for a match wearing his hook, which he then elaborately removed and hung by the curved prongs either on the chain-link fence above the opposing team's bench or more spectacularly on the end of the net where each side passed back and forth repeatedly after a certain number of games. The more prominent the hook was displayed at the onset of the match, the more the opposing team jibed with each other, deciding that they surely had a great chance to beat a twosome in which one of the players was stumpy.

As team captain, Bill had John serve second. By then the opponents were sure the game was theirs, knowing a one-armed guy was at the disadvantage with serving, which is usually a two-handed event. To their amazement John threw up the tennis ball with his good right hand while also holding the racket in the same hand, and as the ball dropped in range he often slammed an ace into the opposing fore court while Bill guffawed from their baseline. It did not take long for their shtick to make the rounds and for opponents to know ahead of time what they were in for, but just for good measure Bill and John always repeated the hook-on-the-net routine with each new match. They became known among local tennis players as Single Wing and Double Wing, and the Wings' shtick soon became legend.

When I married John I did not know how much his prostheses would take on a life of their own. In fact I did not know much about prostheses at all, but it did not take long for me to learn about them. In fact, forty-eight years later I am still learning. Recently he told me that while he was driving our car that morning, he passed a man on a bicycle using a prosthetic leg to pedal the bike. I mentioned that the man must have gone to his prosthetic vendor and asked that a bike-adapted leg be made for him, as I have always thought was true with John and his various prosthetic limbs.

"Oh, no," replied John. "Unless you need some special modification, you just go into the prosthetics office and sit down with a catalogue and pick out the adapted limb that you need."

Depending on his perception of the need for either more physical strength and dexterity or more social in-fitting, the prosthesis-of-the-day might be a two-pronged metal hook attached to a hard-bodied sleeve that fits over the stump of his forearm (strength) or a flesh-toned five-fingered myoelectric hand and forearm complete with fingernails (social) or some variation on one of these devices.

The hook, a hard-working but not very lovely-to-look-at prosthesis, is manually operated by a cable-like system of criss-crossing straps that slip over both shoulders, much like the straps of a double holster. By lifting or lowering a shoulder he can open or close the hook at will. Because the hook does not have any electrically-controlled moving parts, it is a good choice to be worn around water-related events, like fishing or white-water rafting. John has had two kinds of hooks—a so-called farmer hook, named thus because it is useful for people who do heavy outdoor work, like gardening or farming. As far as I know he has never worn his farmer hook.

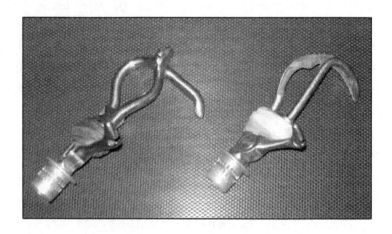

Farmer hook (left) and daily use hook, both reinforced with medical grade bands for extra strength (right). Note shiny newness of farmer hook.

His other hook, a more every day one, has always been ramped up for strength by attaching anywhere from one to four industrial strength rubber bands to the resistance area. When fully engaged it can apply almost thirty pounds per inch of pressure to anything that is between its claws.

The hook is capable of much finely tuned pincing and can lift a single hair or pick up a tissue or it can close tightly around the edge of a heavy object or even a live coal if there is a need to retrieve such an item from a fireplace in the absence of tongs. Occasionally the hook overdoes its gripping facility and crushes a delicate object like the stem of a wine glass or a baby's

tiny finger. John has many variations of the hook prosthesis— like for golf, skiing, tennis, for eating lobster and crab legs, for barbecuing, for heavy-duty lifting— and there are stories about his adventures with each one.

John cooks bacon using both the tongs and his hook to transport the slices to and from the frying pan. 2009

The prosthetic hand is much more esthetically appealing but like many attractive creations, it cannot do much more than look good. It has some prehensile gripping ability but the strength is limited, and it cannot reliably grasp small or delicate objects as can the hook. During the first ten years I knew John, his hook and his hand were interchangeable, both being inserted into the stump casing of a shoulder cable device, and each able to do basically two things—open and close.

In about 1969 the Veteran's Administration (VA) invited him to be one of their first amps to try out a newly developed hand, one that had the advantage of having no shoulder straps or cables, and that could be a better choice for wearing under suits and other formal-type jackets, where most people would hardly even notice its presence. The VA wanted someone who used his prosthesis as a normal armed person would use a regular hand and arm so they could evaluate its strengths and limitations.

John was a good choice for them. He nearly beat that hand to pieces using it for all kinds of activities, and within a few years the VA hand was replaced by a far more complex device, the Otto Bock myoelectric hand, engineered in Germany and designed to be state-of- the art for amputees who need more than a cosmetically appealing hand.

The Otto Bock hard shell prosthesis fits over the stump with a kind of suction developed from wetting the stump and then sliding it into the hollowed-out receptacle. Electrodes contained in the receptacle make direct contact with the skin over the nerve endings in the stump, thus allowing the wearer to think about an action and the electric hand responds by opening or closing itself.

While the Bock myoelectric hand was definitely an improvement over the glorified hook/hand, it is limited by its inability to rotate automatically on the wrist and for the fingers to move independently. In order to pick something up with the Bock hand, the person must hover the hand over the item and think the hand open, then closed, making it apparent to an observer that there is something different about that hand. It also makes a little bit of a motorized sound as the complex mechanisms inside do their jobs of opening and closing. The myoelectric hand also has its limits in social situations where it can be predicted occasionally to close too roughly on a plastic drinking glass sending red wine cascading onto the carpet of hosts. If it is holding a stemmed wine glass, the user has to lift the hand awkwardly in front of his mouth and then lean into the drink in order to sample the fluid, since the wrist does not rotate. Additionally, it cannot be worn in water, like in the shower or in a swimming pool.

In addition to the prosthetic hands, John at one time had a variety of artificial ears. While he was still in rehab at Wilford Hall, he visited the dental lab there where the technicians made a mold of his remaining ear then created a mirror-imaged silicone version of it which was applied as needed to the side of his head, using the same kind of surgical adhesive that people with ostomies use to attach their device.

John with red wine 2009

When we were first married he would from time to time bring out from his dresser a small craft-type package of vials of paint and a brush, like for doing water colors. Then he would apply a little pink or red or brown or yellow paint to the otherwise flesh-colored artificial ear, trying to blend it to match the time of year and his tan factor. When hair fashion changed and he grew his hair longer over his ears in the 1980's, he decided to stop wearing his artificial ear since it was often cumbersome to put it on and the adhesive was sticky and irritated his skin. He never resumed wearing it again, although in the 1990's he considered a newer version of a prosthetic ear, fondly called the Snap-on device. In this case the ear-deprived person has a series of metal protuberates (the so-called male parts) inserted into the skull around the opening to the ear canal. Matching receptacles (female parts) on a silicone replacement ear allow the person to literally snap the ear in place. The manufacturer enthused that all this would be covered by the VA, since John's need for it was a service-connected disability.

"I don't think so," he answered in response to the "go/no go" question. "I didn't get a rug when I started to lose my hair and I think I'll just stay bald-eared."

The latex glove covering the mechanical hand also needs to be matched to his particular skin tone and over time gloves sometimes turn darker than his fair color as a result of exposure to the elements, to imbedded dirt, or to chemical processes within the latex. About eight times a year, John needs to get a glove change, which can be done by a technician in a prosthetics office in a few minutes time. The VA contracts with civilian prosthetic offices to provide the devices and the maintenance thereof. Periodically the hands wear out or technology changes and he needs to get a new hand. As a result we have several boxes of discarded arms and hooks stored in various closets and attics.

Peter W. Rosenberger of Nashville is the president of the Christian-inspired not-for-profit agency, Standing with Hope, Inc., a prosthetic limb outreach he founded with his wife, Gracie, a double leg amputee to whom he has been married for twenty-five years. The Rosenberger's' charity has established a prosthetic limb recycling operation in which they partner with prison inmates who learn how to disassemble the donated limbs and to repurpose them for use in the United States and other countries.

We would like to donate John's arms to this or to another charity but we have learned that since the prosthetic devices are purchased for him by the VA, they are technically owned by the U.S. government and as such cannot be donated. When I get in cleaning-out mode, I pull these boxes of now-unused arms out from the dusty corners where they have been sitting and often have John move them to another nook to free up a little space. Invariably when I see him carrying a box of prosthetic devices wedged between his good arm and his artificial one, I ask him whether he has a permit to carry arms.

೪

Despite our now almost forty-eight years of marriage I have never seen John's prosthesis naked—without a glove covering its intricate mechanizations. I have never gone with him to his prosthetics office when he gets a new glove applied nor have I ever even sneaked a look by peeling back the covering on one of the hands in his closet. It never occurred to me to be curious about such things until the summer of 2014 when we were attending another of the myriad of Amputee Golf Association tourneys in which he has participated over the years.

Prostheses hanging in the closet

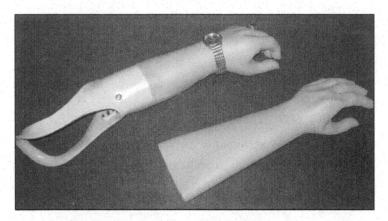

Otto Bock myoelectric hand and new glove

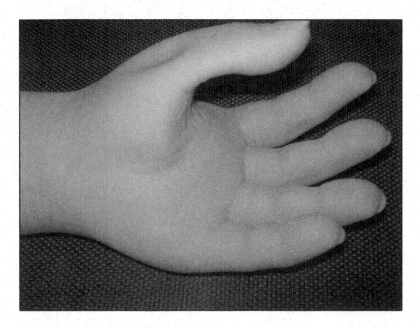

Close up of glove, showing realistic hand wrinkles and fingernails

As we stood in the buffet line for dinner one night, I noticed across the pan of barbecue chicken a man who was holding his plate in an ungloved prosthetic hand. Startled, I couldn't keep my eyes off it. He managed to hold the plate so deftly in the prosthetic device and to have such confidence in being able to swivel his wrist as needed. At the first opportunity I approached the stranger and discreetly asked if I could have a closer look at his buck naked hand. I learned his was not the same bionic hand John had worn for all these years but was a new generation 2014 technologically revolutionized version of the hand worn by Lee Majors in *The Six Million Dollar Man*. This man was also a sales representative for the company and chose to wear his prosthetic without its glove so he could more easily demonstrate its workings when the opportunity arose, sort of like the car salesmen whose floor models have stripped off hood coverings so the engine can more easily be visualized.

For more than thirty years, medical scientists have successfully transplanted donor organs, both from live donors and from cadavers. In some cases micro-surgery techniques have allowed the re-attachment of a patient's own body part that had been cut off either accidentally or intentionally, like with a hand or a penis. Often such dismembering events take place on a battlefield or in a major auto or other vehicular accident where such immediate and precise care cannot be rendered. In order to successfully re-implant such an organ, the cut must have been relatively clean and the organ must be preserved in ice and attached or re-attached as soon as possible.

When nerves and muscles are severed, time is the greatest challenge to surgeons relative to restoration of function. "Nerves typically grow at a rate of only one millimeter per day and muscles develop permanent atrophy after one year, so restoring limb function is a race against time," writes Dagny Stuart. A team of Vanderbilt investigators is studying the possibility of buying time and restoring nerve function though application of polyethylene glycol (PEG), a commonly used and relatively safe solution, that "helps severed nerve stumps stick together and begin to function," says Stuart.

The quest for body parts leads one into areas—like 3D printing—thought only a few years ago to be in the far-off realm of science fiction. Today, however, 3D printing is allowing customized prostheses to be developed for humans and even for ducks. Buttercup was hatched with a backward facing foot. Knowing she could not survive such a handicap, a local veterinarian amputated the foot. Nashville-based NovaCopy created the prototype replacement foot in a 13 1/2 hour printing process, and Buttercup strutted her stuff on national television. 3D technology allowed Bilal Ghalib and others in the U.S to design a custom knee prosthesis for Bilal's cousin in Baghdad, who lost his leg to the effects of diabetes.

From the early 1980's until about 2007 there had been little research or new development into advanced prosthetics because there wasn't much of a market for such devices. As the present wars heated up, the injuries sustained therein were mostly limited to traumatic brain injuries and limb amputations, both caused by IED's. As these vets survived and returned home, Congress finally began noticing and millions of dollars of funds have begun to infuse for development of newer, more efficient prostheses. Additionally biomechanics and development of robotics are becoming mainstream in medical education and in practice allowing the visions of filmmakers thirty years earlier to become reality. Practically every week a story in the news details a new development or some new implement or just the incredible hardiness of folks who have experienced traumatic injuries.

During the 2013 annual meeting of the American Association for the Advancement of Science (AAAS) in Boston, researchers from Switzerland's Ecole Polytechnique Federale de Lausanne (EPFL) unveiled their new prototypical bionic hand that contains wiring connecting it directly into the nervous system of the wearer, allowing the sensation of touch to return to an amputee. The prosthetic hand senses when to tighten and when to loosen grip depending on the object being held.

At the Center for Intelligent Mechatronics at Vanderbilt Medical Center, Dr. Michael Goldfarb, a professor of mechanical engineering, along with a dedicated team of researchers, graduate students, and engineers, are focused on developing "robotic artificial legs and arms for amputees, and robotic lower-limb exoskeletons that will allow paraplegics to walk again." In several recent news stories, Goldfarb's work with high profile amputees, like Craig Hutto, a 23-year old whose story became a YouTube sensation after his leg was bitten off in a shark attack, has highlighted the marriage of computer, sensor, electric motor, and battery technology in ways that allow today's prosthetics to mimic the actual motions made by normally limbed people. In its quest for even better-designed prosthetics that are lighter and quieter than older ones, and in which the control systems are reliable, the Center for Intelligent Mechatronics is "also developing an anthropomorphic prosthetic arm project and an advanced exoskeleton to aid in physical therapy.'

The March 2011 issue of *National Geographic* featured "Miracle Grow," the science-fiction-meets-reality story about progress being made in laboratories worldwide in their quest to regrow human body parts for those 100,000 or so people in the U.S. alone who are waiting for organ transplants. Since waiting for a donor organ to become available is a long and often unsuccessful process, a newer solution is becoming available. "Bioartificial organs" grown from the patient's own cells which can then be spliced into or onto the person's body is the promise of the future. A two-page color photo of the synthetic scaffold of a left ear, sitting in a Petri dish "bathed in cartilage-producing cells, part of a project to grow new ears for wounded soldiers," is the compelling image used in the story to illustrate this amazing new scientific frontier. Princeton

University scientists are growing in Petri dishes ears made with a 3D printer that can "hear" radio frequencies. Describing this research in an Associated Press article in 2013, writer Keith Collins says the field of cyberkinetics, combining biology and technology, may open humans to function beyond the usual five senses, "to a sort of electronic sixth sense," quoting Michael McAlpine, the professor who led the project.

Every war produces grim images of survivors, especially survivors who are amputees. The American Civil War which was the first such combat to be documented by photographs, produced thousands of images of amputees in every battle. If a Union amputee survived, he was granted the benefit of receiving a prosthesis, but if one lost a limb in service to the Confederacy, there was no such aftercare. In a recent traveling Smithsonian Museum exhibition of Civil War memorabilia, I was momentarily stunned to see that the technology for prosthetics in 1865 was roughly the same as that for prosthetics more than

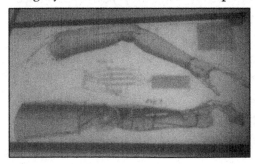

100 years later, as shown in this photograph taken by the author at the exhibition in Nashville.

Responding to very public reports in 2007 of poor conditions in the outpatient care of returning injured veterans of current wars at Walter Reed Army Medical Center, the military created Warrior Transition Units there and elsewhere. Funded through the American Recovery and Reinvestment Act of 2009, the army in late 2011 unveiled its efforts to revamp its medical treatment for ill, injured, or combat wounded soldiers, which included the establishment of new four-story apartment style barracks which opened in October of that year at Fort Campbell Army Base in Kentucky. The barracks house up to 206 soldiers who use wheelchairs or prosthetics or who need specialized medical care, according to a Oct. 12, 2011 news story in the *Tennessean*.

John and I visited the Warriors in Transition barrack at Ft. Campbell in the spring of 2013. Ft. Campbell, a sprawling facility covering almost 160,000 acres, straddles the Kentucky/Tennessee line about fifty-five miles northwest of Nashville. It is the home of the 1st and 3rd Army and of the legendary 101st Airborne Air Assault Division with 31,000 active duty personnel and families and 8,000 civilian employees.

David Twillie, M.D., a fifty-year-old twice-deployed former army doctor who opted out of a third deployment but continues to work in an administrative role with returning soldiers, toured us through the Warriors in Transition facility. Where earlier the battalion's staff was spread out in trailers and other buildings all over the installation, he told us, the new quarters provide recovering soldiers with housing that is close to their unit leadership and also to the Blanchfield Army Community Hospital. The barracks, which more nearly resemble a college style dormitory than an army barrack, provide the soldiers with accessible kitchens, bathrooms, and laundry areas that allow room for wheelchairs, motion sensors on lights, and accessible showers. Outside the barracks is a wheelchair obstacle course which gives recovering soldiers experience in maneuvering their chairs through real-life like inclines and other obstacles.

Dr. Twillie described to us the ways the modern military is helping current returning personnel to remain in their units and to reintegrate with their families after a combat injury.

"It used to be that once the injuries were healed, soldiers were mustered out and said goodbye to their military career. Nowadays, about 90% of the servicemen and women who are injured come back to Ft. Campbell after they are stabilized," Dr. Twillie told us. "Even if someone cannot permanently rejoin their group, it may take one and one-half or two years for eventual separation to occur."

"The thrust of rehabilitation for the current wars is care for amputations and traumatic brain injuries (TBI) as well as psychological issues," he said as we entered the TBI rehabilitation building. Inside the brain training room, we saw recovering vets working in simulators that take them back into warfare step-by-step, allowing them to recover from the post-traumatic stress disorders (PTSD) that accompany almost every combat situation and to master the skills they need to re-enter their military careers.

The May/June 2012, issue of *DAV Magazine* profiles Past DAV (Disabled American Veterans) National Commander, Roberto "Bobby" Barrera, who lost his right hand and his entire left arm in 1969 in Vietnam when his armored personnel carrier was hit by a 500-pound bomb. Barrera, who has worn a right hook all these 43 years, has now been accepted on the waiting list for a hand transplant through Johns Hopkins in Baltimore, MD. He says that with such little focus being placed on upper extremity amputations, he never expected a full hand transplant would be possible. Showing the humor that undoubtedly helped him overcome his initial injuries, he philosophically remarks that should the surgery fail to succeed he's just be back to where he has been for most of his life.

In the same article, the role of facial reconstructive surgery, including the ability to do a complete facial transplant, is highlighted. A photo is included showing a Marine captain in 2010 at Lackland AFB being fitted with an ear prosthesis similar to the one John received. Other veterans have benefited from Faces of Honor and Operation Mend, pro bono programs that provide "reparative facial work for wounds suffered in combat." (p 18)

On a visit to San Antonio in 2005, John and I played a round of golf together at Gateway Hills, the military golf course at Lackland AFB. Lackland used to be a separate air force base, but today it is part of the Joint Base San Antonio, an amalgamation of the United States Army Fort Sam Houston, the United States Air Force Randolph Air Force Base, and Lackland Air Force Base, which were merged in October 2010. Wilford Hall Hospital is now called the 59th Medical Wing.

John remembers as a patient at Wilford Hall looking out a window and seeing the golf course. Since then he has returned and played at Gateway several times with former military buddies. The course is like an oasis on the grounds of the otherwise all business facility, situated just off Military Drive. The ninth hole plays up a steep hill and as we made the turn, John pointed off in the distance to a large creamy peach concrete building, saying "That is Wilford Hall Hospital."

Leaving the TBI building after we separated from Dr. Twillie, John looked at me and said, "When I was at Wilford Hall, I didn't have family around me after the crisis passed. I just went out and did my thing—what I needed to do."

We smiled and shook our heads to think about how different his experience might be today.

What's funny about being an amp?

Humor has always been used to diffuse tension, whether the tension of everyday activities or that of war-time living. In fact, almost all accounts of survival in the face of adversity cite a sense of humor as one of the essential characteristics as a predictor of success. Some humor is directed externally—poking fun at one's adversaries—and some is inner directed—laughing at oneself. In this era of politically correct humor, it is sometimes seen as insensitive to laugh at someone or something that is challenged or disabled as many people over the age of forty were taught to call such circumstances.

Amputee humor requires a strong stomach, not just because some of the jokes are so gut-wrenchingly awful and insensitive, but also because some of them are gut-busting hilarious. Josh Sundquist, a leg-amputee as a result of childhood cancer and author of the national bestseller *Just Don't Fall: How I Grew Up, Conquered Illness, and Made It Down the Mountain* (Penguin Group, 2010), hosts a "best amputee jokes contest" at his blog www.lessthanfour.org.

Wolf, an arm amputee and the third-place winner in Sundquist's 2010 jokes contest, says, "Disability humor seems to evoke both fear and joy, both embarrassment and slapstick. Never is disability humor outright tasteful. It often seems to play with stereotypes. There always is a degree of 'hoops' involved... But of all the disability jokes, this one brings it to a point: a woman puts out an ad for the guy with the most incredible sex powers ever. When the door rings, she finds a guy without arms or legs sitting in a wheelchair is waiting in front of her door. When she asks him, 'What are you doing here?' He answers, 'Well I'm here for your ad in the paper.' She asks, 'So how did you imagine this would go?' He replied, 'Well how do you imagine I rang the doorbell?' "

From time to time Internet-circulated jokes about disarmed people make their way into my inbox. One of the more recent ones had to do with a one-armed man who was contemplating suicide until he saw a no-armed man, running and dancing along, appearing to be exquisitely happy. Seeing him, the first man changed his mind and climbed down from the perilous height from which he had intended to jump. He caught up with the other man, inquiring how he could be so seemingly happy when he had no arms, to which the man replied, "I'm not happy at all. I'm moving along like this because I can't reach down and scratch my balls."

Why is this joke funny enough to keep circulating, and un-funny enough to cause a shudder? All jokes take hold because there is both an element of truth and an element of fear in them. No one wants to lose an arm, much less two arms, or two legs but at the same time all men—and women, too—can relate to how good it feels to scratch whatever itches.

I have learned from spending almost fifty years in association with amputees—both arm and leg, and combat and non-combat-related causes—that among the fraternity members and their spouses, almost any kind of humor, even very-dark stuff, is okay, but from outside, it may come across as insensitive. John, however, does not seem to have a sensitive bone in his body when it comes to giving and getting arm, hand, or ear-related humor. Whether it is an unintentionally funny "Buddy, can I give you a hand with that?" from someone who sees him struggling to load luggage in the overhead container in an airplane ("Sure, I'd appreciate that since I only have one of my own") or "Hey, John, can you lend me a hand?" ("Okay, but it may not fit you too well") or "Can I bend your ear a moment about something?" ("Yes, but be careful because it could fall off"), John has never gotten his back up by anything that is said about his state of disarmament.

Recently I posted a vacation photo to friends and family, some of whom said, maybe a little tongue in cheek, that I have a wicked sense of humor. In the photo taken by a friend, we are seated poolside next to each other in beach recliners. I am on John's left side sipping a drink which I am holding in my left hand and I am holding his prosthesis with my right hand, as though offering it to him. In the artificial hand is a plastic drinking glass with a straw emerging from the top of the glass. John is leaning over to drink from it, his left arm stump parked at his side. I captioned the photo, "The ultimate vacation indulgence. Giving

John a hand with his drink." He laughed longest and loudest.

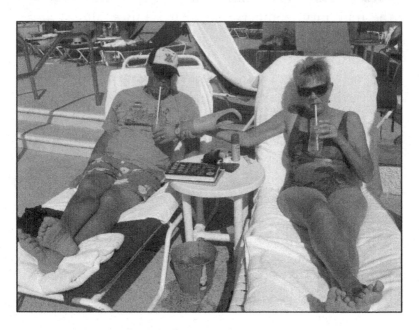

Giving John a hand with his drink.

Washington Post reporter Christian Davenport has written about the dark humor used by amputee veterans of our current wars as they bond and heal during their months-long rehabilitation program at Walter Reed Army Medical Center. Noting that the uneducated public, not really knowing what to say or do usually stares at and/or pities a vet who is an amp, Davenport chronicles how some amps use humor to diffuse these situations. Describing the story of Pat Murray, an Iraq war veteran whose prosthetic leg usually gets attention and maybe also *"that look"* (quote and italics by Davenport), the writer says Murray adapts by striking first. Murray may see a woman putting her hand into the space between a closing elevator door at the same time as he is approaching the elevator. Pointing to his own missing leg he will say to her, "Careful, you can lose a limb that way." When the woman withdraws her hand and tries to get her mind around the facts of his absent leg and her now-safe hand, Murray "flashes a smile, chuckles, and suddenly the ride up isn't nearly so awkward after all." (*Washington Post*, July 30, 2009)

Sometimes such humor can be considered bizarre or twisted to an outsider but it is a crucial part of the amputee's defense mechanisms and to their sense of well-being. Davenport notes, "(t)he sphere of people who can get away with telling amputee jokes is tightly defined, and not every wounded warrior is able to joke about having a hard time going up stairs or holding a cup of coffee. But for others, it's the ultimate palliative as they move from denial to anger to acceptance."

Davenport reports that veteran amps at Walter Reed call other amps special names, like Five, for the number of fingers left for an amp with one arm missing, and Gimpy or Peg-leg for those with leg amputations. The Walter Reed amps have printed up business cards or tee shirts mocking their situations, with sayings like "Buy a Marine. 25-50 percent off. Some assembly required," and "Dude, where's my leg." Or darkest of all, "I went to Iraq, lost my leg, and all I got was this T-shirt."

The leg amp vets at Walter Reed created a Top Ten list of positive things about being a double leg amputee, like "You can always wear shorts," and "Your feet don't smell." John's Top Ten list for being a single arm amputee, with a bonus for having a missing ear, includes, "You get half price on manicures," "You never wear out both gloves in an expensive leather pair," "You only need to spend money for one hearing aid," "You can instantly lose six pounds by removing your artificial arm," "Your hook may leave you hanging, but at least you will be alive," and my favorite, "You can remove a broken-off light bulb from its socket without needing to go look for pliers."

Presenting at the TED conference in Vancouver in March 2014, Dr. Hugh Herr, a double leg amputee and patent-holder for numerous prosthetic devices, described autobiographically his experience with early prosthetics that "allowed him to adjust his height from 5 feet to 6 1/2 feet plus. '(When I was feeling badly about myself, insecure, I would jack my height up...but when I was feeling confident and suave, I would knock my height down a notch, just to give the competition a chance.')" (*Smithsonian*, November 2014)

John and his buddies, especially his golf and other sports buddies, have long used humor with each other as an end run around being amputees. Among the leg and arm amputees with whom he competes in the National Amputee Golf Association circuit, amp jokes can turn very dark.

One time his buddy, John Bragan, now-deceased, a double leg amp with one below-knee stump and one above-knee stump, had removed his prosthetic legs in the motel room after a round. John M knocked on his door to go to dinner and John B, having not yet replaced his artificial legs, hobbled to the door, stumbling unevenly on his leg stumps. When the door opened John M looked into the room over the much shorter John B's head and said, "Bragan, where are you?"

Looking up, John B answered, "Down here," to which John M responded, "Oh, hell, it's bad enough to have to eat dinner with all these amps, but I didn't know I was going to have to eat dinner with a dwarf, too."

I have never known John to engage in self pity. There are times when he is clearly frustrated to not have use of both hands as he would prefer, but in almost every situation he adapts, finding some way to accomplish with one hand and a hook or artificial hand, what everyone else does with two hands. He does often get stares when in new situations with strangers and especially from children, whose parents may try to shush or re-direct the child, as though their curiosity might somehow confirm the absence of his arm and silence will keep the situation at bay.

Perhaps unlike some people who have disabilities, John has always welcomed questions from children and from anyone else. If the other person is also capable of joining him in some good-natured amp humor, that person is likely to be a friend for a long time. Sometimes he seems to be so able bodied that he truly seems to be unaware that he has a missing limb. Recently, as I was reviewing with him some of my notes for this book, he looked at me, quite seriously, and said, "Am I really an amputee?" Not quite knowing at the moment whether he was serious or joking, I replied, "Yes, John, you have been an amputee for almost fifty years."

Amps and athletes

Today it is commonplace to see able bodied and disabled athletes compete alongside one another, but that has not always been so. If a person lost a limb forty or fifty years ago, most people thought that person's athletic competitions were automatically ended. From somewhat regular-appearing stories of junior high and high school athlete's return to competition after amputations to the Blade Runner's appearance in the 2012 Olympics to Adrianne Haslet-Davis, who lost her leg to the bomb detonated at the Boston Marathon in 2013 and then who dazzled on Dancing with the Stars in 2014, there is now no doubt about the ability of true athletes, with or without natural limbs, to compete at every level of sports.

Some athletes have even found themselves a leg up, so to speak, after becoming amputees. Hugh Herr, now a PhD and holder of numerous patents in biomechatronics, lost both legs in a climbing accident when he was seventeen. Wearing prostheses he designed he returned to the rock faces he had previously climbed and found he could actually climb better in the prostheses than when he was naturally limbed. (*Smithsonian* November 2014. Giant Steps by Matthew Shaer).

Just outside Tacoma, Washington, American Lake Veterans Golf Course, a nine-hole facility restricted to play only by veterans, their guests, and employees of the Veterans' Administration, opened in 1956 on the grounds of the VA Puget Sound Health Care System. It "is the nation's only golf course designed specifically for the rehabilitation of wounded and disabled veterans. At this unique facility disabled veterans can hit balls, take lessons and play the course. Blind golfers, amputees, and veterans recovering from emotional trauma and other injuries can join able-bodied soldiers, sailors, airmen and marines for camaraderie, support and rounds of golf – all in an atmosphere of honor and acceptance."

American Lake broke ground in August, 2013 on a second nine holes, designed to be completely handicap accessible. Jack Nicklaus, the PGA's most prolific golfer, who has designed courses in every part of the globe, has volunteered his time to design this new course and to modify the original course. The $4.5 million renovation project is called "A Course in Courage: Healing America's Veterans through Golf." When it opens in 2015 there will be handicap accessible bunkers and greens, larger tee boxes, and specially modified carts that allow leg and arm amputee vets to play the game almost as they did before they were injured.

Golf has become the go-to athletic activity for rehabilitation of amputees from the current wars. Writing in the online edition of *The Atlantic* in April, 2012, Timothy Bella describes the work being done at the Adaptive Golf Academy in Tampa. "For a game that has been historically important for returning amputee war veterans, the sport continues to be a crucial rehab tool, a refuge for the recent wave of 20-something veterans and active-duty soldiers from Iraq and Afghanistan looking to regain some semblance of regular civilian life." Bella profiles 25 year-old Joel Tavera, a totally blind leg and partial-hands amputee vet who is facing his 77th post-injury surgery. Tavera is beginning to play golf and is joking, "likening his golf game to Tiger Woods sans the women," writes Bella.

John had played golf before his accident, but it was not until about seven years after he lost his arm, when we were living in Nevada, that he started playing again, holding the club in his right hand and bracing his stump on the shaft of the club as he made his full golf swing. Anyone who has ever had a golf lesson has probably learned early-on the importance of the non-dominant hand and arm in powering through the swing. Most golf involves a little wagering. The normies whose foursome in Nevada included John would size him up and quickly take his bet, wondering after they had lost their dollars to him after a round if they might have been fleeced by a one-arm-bandit that was not in a casino.

He first learned about the National Amputee Golf Association (NAGA) after we moved to Tennessee, and he immediately entered the National Tournament, played that year on four different courses at Pinehurst, North Carolina. It only took him one round at Pinehurst to learn that his game was nowhere near the game of the amputee men and women against whom he was competing. He limped home with no trophy and promptly found a prosthetic vendor who had already designed a golf hand for another amputee golfer, a woman, and had the man design for him a similar one—a variation on a hook prosthesis, without cables and without the two claws.

John prepares to tee off. Brentwood Country Club. C. 2009

The golf hand has a three-inch long C-curved tapered metal adaptive piece through which the grip of a club can pass and wedge securely in place. This adapter attaches to the unit with a pin through a universal joint that is soldered into a hard-shelled casing which fits over the stump. Velcro straps secure the apparatus above the bend in the elbow. With this prosthesis John could now grasp the shaft of his golf club with his left hand and feel the powering through movement that had been missing from his game up until then.

The next year he won his division of the Tennessee amputee golf championship. Since 1976 he has competed almost every year on the NAGA state, regional, national, and international circuits, winning his division at all levels at one time or another. In 2010 he played on the NAGA College Park Cup team, their version of the Ryder Cup, contributing his singles match win to the overall United States sweep of that bi-annual event.

In 1983 he was sponsored to play as the only amp on the four-person team that won the pro-am of the then-named Georgia-Pacific Atlanta Golf Classic. His team, playing with Canadian golf pro Dan Halldorson, defeated teams headed by Craig Stadler, Gary Player, Lou Graham, Tom Watson, J.C. Snead, Al Geiberger, Raymond Floyd, Larry Ziegler, Fred Couples, Tom Weiskopf, and others.

But it is in the casual day in, day out play on his home course where most of the stories have gotten traction, like the one from the 1980's where his buddy, Mike, on observing the oversize Jack Nicklaus

Response putter he was using at that time, said, "John, it looks like you just kept holding on to the joy stick after they wouldn't put you back in the pilot's seat."

Georgia-Pacific Atlanta Golf Classic
PRO-AM May 16, 1983

John and his winning team

Today, unfortunately there are several newly-retired first lieutenants from our country's current combat theaters, but at age seventy-three, John is one of a handful of aging retired first lieutenants from the Vietnam era. He proudly joins with his same-aged peers, whose careers took them to commander or colonel or admiral or general rank, in being a staunch supporter of the military men and women who keep our country safe. Whenever he is asked to do so, he shares his story with any of today's combat veterans who have also lost a limb, bringing his strength, hope, and experience to their lives. And he continues to compete in sports events against both fully-limbed (called normies by the amputee community) and differently-limbed (called amps by the normie community) athletes—usually competing at the highest level and often defeating both normies and other amps.

The early years

For the first three years of our marriage John and I seemed to be in perpetual motion, having two children twenty-one months apart, and starting then ending six jobs between us. We moved from our initial efficiency to a larger Chicago apartment, then for a year to an apartment in Milwaukee, until John decided he could not see a future for himself selling light industrial equipment. After fruitless attempts to find a job in which he could be a pilot or something else, we then

moved back to Chicago where we experienced our first episode of home-lessness and jobless-ness, camping out for several months on the sofa of his dad's apartment with our toddler daughter. By then our second child was on the way.

John gives a hand to Elizabeth c. 1969

Finally three months before the birth of our son and through the help of a college friend of mine, John got a job working as plant operations manager for a crushed stone mining operation in a suburb of Chicago. We moved first into a second floor two-bedroom garden apartment, then after the arrival of our son, into a three bedroom apartment across the hall, which was probably less than eight-hundred square feet in total space. John seemed to relish this work, which involved among other things operating heavy equipment, like loaders and dozers, and for a while I thought he had found himself a new career.

In 1972, however, chasing a childhood dream as yet unknown to me, John quit his job at the crushed stone operation where he had worked for two and a half years. We decided to move to northeastern Nevada, where we had previously visited on a junket out of Chicago designed to entice new residents to settle in the high desert community of Spring Creek then being developed outside Elko by chain-saw magnate and entrepreneur, Robert P. McCulloch. McCulloch had recently moved the London Bridge from England to Lake Havasu, Arizona, which everyone had declared to be a folly, and conventional wisdom was that Spring Creek would be another boondoggle.

Spring Creek was virtually undeveloped when we first saw it, but that did not stop us from writing a check for the down payment on a one-acre lot and pointing our sights west in search of Utopia. We loaded our possessions in a U-Haul truck and caravanned across the Midwest on Interstate 80, then moved into a rental house in a nice residential neighborhood in the small town of Elko, ten miles from Spring Creek. While I did not share the same dream as John's, moving into a home was a partial wish come true, since we had been living in walk-up cramped apartments, and now we actually had a yard in which the children could play.

We had only lived in Elko for a few weeks when John needed to get a haircut. Finding someone new to cut my hair is an involved process requiring that I ask among friends, seek references, and even visit the salon before I go to get a feel for the place. For John, it just involves walking into the first place where a barber pole is revolving and sitting down to wait his turn.

In the 1970's Elko was a town split in half by the original transcontinental railroad tracks laid more than a hundred years earlier to carry goods and passengers between the developing western United States and the more settled eastern part of the country. From its beginnings, Elko had been a train town, a ranch community, and the biggest locale for casinos in all of northeastern Nevada. The two major casinos were in downtown Elko, one on either side of the tracks.

The Commercial Hotel and Casino, on the northern side of the tracks, was famous for having on display in its foyer a stuffed polar bear in full standing position. Touring singing groups from all over the country stopped from time to time to play the stage at the Commercial, hoping a few gamblers would take a break and enjoy their music. Locals could almost always count on seeing The Matys Brothers, a second tier singing duo, in the lounge every week.

The Stockmen's Hotel and Casino, a more modern establishment than the Commercial, was across the tracks on the southern side, an easy walk from Idaho Street, the main highway that paralleled the railroad tracks through town, and from the brothels located one street further south behind the Stockmen's.

Prostitution was allowed in Nevada by local option, and Elko County, which had a population of about 15,000 people in 1970, had five brothels—Sue's, Rosie's, Betty's, Inez's, and Mona's. John's first job in Elko was selling cars at the local Ford/Lincoln/Mercury dealership, and his best customers were the madams, who loved their brand new Lincoln Continentals. These business women often had separate private homes in the town proper, and the house we rented in Elko, and then eventually bought, was owned by Rosie. For several of the years we lived in Rosie's house, we stored her vintage slot machines and other tools of her business in our basement. When the children began telling their friends about these implements, we asked her to move them out.

Customers on their way to visit one of the whore houses often stopped to get a haircut and a shave at the only barbershop in downtown Elko, located behind the Stockmen's. They waited their turn while sitting in straight backed chairs along the wall next to the local businessmen and ranchers, flipping through girlie magazines or old issues of *Argosy*. Regulars chatted with the lone barber, comparing weather this time of year with that in years past or discussing the spread for the weekend NFL football games.

When it was John's turn for a seat in the chair, he greeted the barber, waited for the cloth to be draped around his torso, and asked for a close cut with a razor finish. The barber barely nodded, continuing to banter with the regulars while going round the top of John's head with scissors then picking up a straight edge barber razor to finely trim the fringe. He folded the right ear and neatly layered the hair ends then turned to the left side, folding that ear to get a better angle. Suddenly the entire artificial ear popped off the side of John's head and tumbled to the floor, where it lay upright amid tufts of hair from earlier customers.

The barber uttered an expletive and took a half step back, and all the customers went silent, gazing at the ear on the floor. Eyes shot back and forth as the men turned to see how much blood was surely spurting from this unknown customer's head. The barber stood frozen in place, razor in hand, his face pale and sweat glistening on his forehead.

John leaned over and looked down at the floor, then peered up at the man, and said, "Well, damn, now you've gone and cut my ear off. And I guess you'll want a tip, too."

The Ruby Mountains of northeastern Nevada, part of the enormous Great Basin of the western United States, run north-southwest for some eighty miles, predominantly in Elko County. The origins of their name vary from historian to historian, but when we lived in Elko, we believed they were named the Rubies because in late winter afternoons, when they were covered in snow, their color would transform from grey or white to brilliant crimson as the setting sun reflected off their western sides. It was a daily miracle to see this color fest, and it was always more beautiful if viewed from the summit of the Lamoille Highway, leading south from Elko past Spring Creek and directly in to the Rubies.

John was born a century too late. He should have ridden a horse for the cavalry or scouted for the settlers or somehow wandered this vast western landscape a hundred years ago, before settlement had changed it. There are places in the Rubies, however, at altitudes above 10,000 feet, where it can seem no one has ever been before, especially if you are on horseback and there is hardly anyone else around.

Cliff and John hunted deer and mountain lions in these mountains for all of the four years we lived nearby. Even forty years after we moved away from there, they periodically have returned to hunt for deer and to fly fish, or in Cliff's case nowadays, to just shoot photographs. Cliff was an Air Force pilot in his younger days, but he and John did not meet until they were in California, each in another phase of life.

Cliff was about five feet seven inches tall, somewhat thick in the middle, balding and with a beard, resembling a gnome more than anything else. John was over six feet tall, dark haired, clean shaven, and relatively trim, even though the two of them actually weighed almost the same. As soon as they saw one another they knew they had been separated at birth. John called Cliff "Midget" and he called John "Stumpy."

They had ridden all day out of base camp in Lamoille Canyon, John atop a quarter horse mare and Cliff on a gelding. Like the men, the horses had to be in good shape for the altitude and for the extra weight they carried on their backs. Most of the time while they were riding the men did not converse very much, but at breaks they would carry on, poking good-humored fun at each other. Riding single file after lunch, they approached a narrow path around the side of a cliff, and both men dismounted to lead their horses over the dangerous pathway.

John led the way, holding the reins of his horse in his right hand, and proceeding very carefully as the shale slid sideways under his boots. A two-foot wide crevice separated one side of the path from the other, and John easily loped over the gap. On the other side he bent to look down the cavity and saw only the narrowest of ledges about six feet down, before a 1000 foot sheer drop. He urged his steed across but she was having none of it, balking also when he yanked hard on the reins.

Cliff decided to help the girl out and he slapped her hard on the flanks, to which assault she bolted, jumping the notch and heading for John's arms. In a split second John decided that the differences in his chances of surviving the onslaught of a nine-hundred pound horse in full flight and of surviving a fall down the crevice were almost none, so he let go of the reins and slid into the crevice. His boots bounced off the sides and his arms were forced upward. At about three seconds in to the fall, he felt a jerk on his left arm and looking up he saw that his hook had grabbed the edge of the crevice, dangling him over the open space.

He hung there for a long moment, bracing his boots against the narrow rocky outcropping and using his right hand to pick out a little piece of solid material to which he could further attach. Looking up he saw Cliff peering down at him, laughing uncontrollably, and he said, "Midget, what the hell did you do that for?"

"It got her over that hole didn't it, Stumpy," Cliff answered, extending his arms and hands to meet John's one hand, eventually helping leverage him up out of the crevice.

On another trip, Cliff and John drove from Elko to the base of Lamoille Canyon, arriving there at about 4:00 AM. It was pitch black and the headlights on Cliff's truck made out a lone horse trailer in the parking lot, where a packer they had hired was unloading two saddled horses and a mule, packed with supplies for their several days long trip. As John prepared to mount his horse in the dark, he slipped his pointed boot into the left stirrup and grabbed the saddle horn with his hook. He began feeling for the reins with his right hand as he started to spring up into the saddle. Just as his hand grabbed the reins, his foot slipped forward in the stirrup, spurring the horse, which took off like a bolt of lightning, carrying the half mounted John on a wild ride like those portrayed in western movies where a cowboy is hanging off the side of a galloping steed. His hook was firmly attached to the horn and wouldn't release. After carrying John along the length of the parking lot, the horse slowed a bit as he reached the trail head. Finally John was able to slip his boot back a notch and the horse immediately stopped, allowing him to pull on up and sit in the saddle, and the hunting trip commenced.

The pack mule, a 600 pound cantankerous muddy-colored work creature whose obsession was in doing exactly what it wanted to do and doing nothing John wanted it to do, had consumed way too much of John's time on the ascension to their first night camp. In the campsite, Cliff and John laid out a rope corral for their horses and put the mule in with the other four-legged animals, which seemed to satisfy the herd instincts for all three beings. Tiring of the mule's antics on the trail, John decided to leave the uncooperative animal behind in the corral as the twosome rode out the next day. They had only gotten about one hundred yards from camp when the mountains began vibrating with the brays of the now lonely penned-in mule.

"Stumpy, you have to go back and get your friend," Cliff told John. "We'll never be able to track anything with that racket going on."

John tied a leader line to the ornery mule and secured it around his hook, then took the reins in his right hand and started back up the trail to Cliff with the mule following behind. Coming through the woods the trail was bisected by a small copse of aspens, a few of their golden leaves still hanging to the branches. John directed his horse to the right side of the fork, and the mule decided it would take the left fork, yanking John backwards out of the saddle.

Cliff came back down the trail to see what was causing even more braying, now accompanied also by human cursing. Meeting John's rider-less horse on the trail, he picked up its reins and hurried on, with the horse following him. He halted mid-step when he found John lying on the trail to the right edge of the aspens. He could see the leader line was still wrapped around the hook and stretched tightly around the trees. Stretching in his saddle to peer around the leftward path, Cliff saw the mule happily grazing on low brush.

Stroking his beard, Cliff sat back in the saddle and said, "Stumpy, I can't quite make out which of you two looks like the biggest jackass."

♎

As a nurse it was always fairly easy for me to find a job staying within my chosen career so I found work at Elko General Hospital, first on the graveyard shift, then later on the 3-11 shift so John could care for the children after school and until their bedtime. In Elko, he worked first as a car salesman, then as a start-up small business entrepreneur, and finally as the owner of an acupuncture clinic—the first in the United States, following Nixon's historic China visit.

The small business endeavor and the acupuncture clinic went belly up, so he moved to Reno, lived in the Rescue Mission, and drove a taxi, while I kept working in the small Elko hospital, 300 miles east of Reno. We defaulted on our property in Spring Creek and in the summer of 1975 we sold most of our possessions in a yard sale. Loading the only furniture we kept—our bedroom set—into a U-Haul trailer which John tethered to the back of our car, we started back across the U.S., headed for Tennessee where I had family and maybe we would find prospects for starting over. We took the southern route—Interstate 40—for this jaunt, staying in Motel Sixes and cooking hot dogs over campfires in state parks. Our children thought it was a great adventure in being pioneers. We lived with relatives and in cheap motels that summer, nearly making ends meet with his Air Force retirement pay and the little money I had withdrawn from a pension plan, but there seemed to be nothing positive on the horizon.

Then one day, while I was attending a nursing seminar in Nashville, I heard about a Master's Degree in Business Administration (MBA) that was available through the then-University of Tennessee, Nashville. They had funds available for eligible veterans to cover tuition, books, and a small stipend. I alerted John, who visited their admissions office, who in turn contacted the Veterans Administration. Checking his records, they told him he had only thirty days left to use the Vocational Rehab dollars for which he was eligible, but they had never really had someone with his level of injury apply for and be successful in a master's level program. They hurried the papers through the system and within a month John was provisionally admitted to the graduate program.

His undergraduate degree in history did not give him the accounting and economics courses he needed for admission, but the funds could be used to provide those classes and in early September he enrolled. In 1977, two years later, after completing the prerequisite and graduate business courses, he received his MBA. There were no Internet social networks available then, so he mailed out about one hundred cover letters and resumes and was hired as Personnel Manager at IKG Industries, division of Harsco Corporation, a fiberglass and steel manufacturing company based in Nashville. We celebrated his finally having a real job on the eve of our tenth wedding anniversary.

ꙮ

The Hiwassee River of western North Carolina and southeastern Tennessee is not famous for its rapids. Nearby streams, like the Ocoee, site of the Olympic kayaking event in 1996, and the Chattahoochee, where *Deliverance* was filmed in the 1970's, are much more notorious. Nevertheless, for a family with a seven and a nine year old child, the Hiwassee was a good place to try rafting for the first time. We had previously tried and enjoyed canoeing as a family on the Harpeth Scenic River near our Middle Tennessee home, and if this new-found Sunday afternoon venture were a success, maybe we would later enjoy rafting the Class Four Nantahala, the Class Five Ocoee, and the Class Six Gauley and New Rivers in West Virginia.

It was about a three hour drive from our home to the place on the Hiwassee where we put in. We parked the car at the registration hut and after signing the requisite waivers we were bussed with eight or ten other people upriver and given a rudimentary lesson in balancing on a rubber raft. Because our children were small enough that they could not reliably assist in operation of the raft, we were assigned two separate vessels, with an adult and a child in each one. We wore our swimsuits with old tee shirts on top and old sneakers on our feet. Everyone was fitted with a life vest, and the adults were given a paddle.

"Now folks, all you really have to know about these rafts is that you need to keep the heavier person sitting on the rim of the stern, and you need to use your paddles only as rudders. The current will do the work and you'll float along at a steady pace," our instructor told us.

The rafts were pulled up on the edge of the river and as we boarded, with John and our daughter in one and me and our son in the other, the operator gave us a push in to the water and we were off.

"There's really no rapids to speak of, but just keep your eyes open in case you go over a rock where the water may dam up and be a little more swift as you crest," the instructor told us as we set off down river.

John does not have a paddle-adapted prosthesis. As with many situations like this where two hands are better than one, he wears his all-purpose double-claw hook, tightened down with several extra-strong medical grade rubber bands, which increase the grip strength on the hook. Grasping the paddle with his right hand near the top, he then firmly attached the hook to the shaft of the oar, and began to steer the raft from his position astern. He placed his feet in the floor of the raft to brace himself. Our daughter sat in the bow, facing her dad.

I adopted the same position in my raft and floated alongside John's raft. The water was no more than a few feet deep at any spot, and the bottom of the river was smooth, so there seemed to be no danger as we moved along. *Besides,* I thought, *John has rescued lots of folks from the Atlantic during his years as a lifeguard.*

He must have heard my thought because he said, "I'd feel better if you'd keep a little in front of me. That way if you get in any trouble I can help you out."

Other rafts with people from our tour as well as several folks who must have put in with other operators floated alongside us and we made idle chat with them, then depending on their whims, they might back off or pass us by. There was no rush, since this was not a race, and the sheer joy of being and not doing was beginning to grow on me. It was easy to get careless about staying braced on the stern and about watching for hidden obstacles in the water, and I had to concentrate to keep the rudder movements on track.

Suddenly I heard John yell. As I looked back I could see the tiniest bit of rapid water coming around the rock he had just hit. I expected to see his raft crest the rock and whiz on past us, which I knew would be an adrenaline surge for him, if not for our daughter. Instead, the jolt tossed him backwards off the raft, and I could see his knees still bent over the edge while his sneakered feet were still inside the boat. His paddle headed towards me and I grabbed it as it started to pass by.

I could see our daughter still sitting in the bow, stretching her neck to try to see her dad but apparently remembering the admonition of the instructor, who had told us to never stand up in the raft. I tried to steer my raft to the water's edge where I might be able to stop but the current kept us moving, albeit slower and in a sideways motion as I shifted the rudder flat against the current. John's raft came up almost alongside mine, and our son, who could now see his dad clearly as he lay in the water behind his raft, shouted, "Mom, look. Dad's lost his arm."

Other floaters nearby heard what the boy had said and they began to abandon their crafts, walking and running through the water towards us to offer their aid. By then I could reach out and grab John's raft and pull my own next to it. His life vest pulled his chest upwards in an awkward arch. He was muttering and cursing, and I was relieved to see he was conscious. The tip of his stump protruded from the water like a short flesh-toned flag pole. While his upper body remained in the water, his legs were still folded over the back of the raft, with the tips of his sneakers dancing up and down one at a time as he tried to stay attached.

I could see he was repeatedly wrapping his right arm and hand across his chest and around his left shoulder, trying to untangle the harness of the prosthesis which had twisted around behind him. The hard shell casing of the device was hanging off the bend of his elbow at a ninety-degree angle above his head.

Replaying this scene in my mind, I don't know which is funnier, the looks on the faces of the Good Samaritans when they realized they were *not* witnessing a re-enactment of the gruesome river scene in *Deliverance* or the sight of John trying to get himself back in that raft in such a state of dissemblance.

ॐ

IKG promoted John at appropriate intervals, giving him more and more opportunity to manage their labor contracts and health care benefits programs. In 1982 he decided to give law school another try, taking the LSAT again, and this time he was accepted in the Nashville School of Law, a program designed for Tennessee residents who worked full-time and who attended classes in the evening.

Law school was arduous, but with the help of his study group, he gutted it out, taking classes half-time his last year so he could be more involved in the activities of our then-high-school-aged children, and he graduated in 1987. He continued to work for IKG, eventually becoming a corporate vice-president of human resources and in-house counsel and taking on more responsibility for their international programs. One of those programs was in Mexico, with operations both in Mexico City and in Querétaro, a city of over a million people several hours north of Mexico City.

John had studied six years of Spanish in high school and college and the vocabulary he accumulated years ago came back rather quickly, enabling him to conduct business speaking the native tongue of the employees, which endeared him to them. But it was outside of the workplace that he made his biggest impression on the Mexican employees, who admiringly called him *El Capitan Gancho*—Captain Hook. When he could do so, he visited the *monumental y querida Plaza de Toreros* in Mexico City, partaking of the bullfights there on Sunday afternoons along with several thousand other fans.

He thrilled to the artistry of veteran *toreros*, like E. Lopez "*El Zotoluco*," and Humberto Flores, as well as the efforts of apprentices (*novilladas)* like "*El Biafra*" and "*El Glison.*" The latter, whose Irish surname is Gleason, made a name for himself in the late 1980's and early 1990's as a man who played by his own rules, eschewing traditional pink stockings which he considered unmanly and using antics from his earlier days as a rodeo clown to entertain the spectators. According to *El Glison's* biography on the Internet, he was old—aged twenty-five—when he decided to become a torero, and he thrived on adventure.

Some of John's Mexican cohorts did not appreciate the *matadores* as did their North American buddy, but they accommodated his interest by introducing him to a local *torero amigo*, Gerardo Peña San Román. Gerardo trained in Coroneo Guanajuato near Querétaro, at a ranch famous for raising fighting bulls, the female offspring of which were nearly as fierce as the males and which were often used in the training ring. The Mexican hosts drove John to the rancho, staying safely out of harm's way in the bleachers when Gerardo invited John to join him in the ring. John did not have a bullfight-adapted prosthesis, but that small detail did not interfere with him accepting Gerardo's invitation, resetting his myoelectric hand with the palm down just before entering the bull ring.

John paid rapt attention as Gerardo demonstrated the fine skill of setting the cape and evading the horns, a mounted picador in the background ready to add a spear to the shoulder of the already insanely angry instrument of death hurtling toward Gerardo. Apparently Gerardo approved of John's skills because the next thing anyone knew, *El Capitan Gancho*, the newest-to-be of the 1993 season's *novilladas* and surely a compatriot of *El Glison*, was alone in the ring with a very angry four-hundred pound fully horned cow running straight towards him, no mercy in her eyes, as the picador stood guard. Who knows what that girl thought of this blue-jean-garbed gringo wearing a baseball cap and an artificial arm adorned with his college logo wristwatch who expertly threw the red cape while she raced under it, rubbing her bleeding forequarter against his trunk?

John in the training ring near Guanajuato, Mexico, c. 1993.

John decided, wisely, that age fifty was a little old to change professions again. Even with his great legs, I really don't think he would have looked very good in pink tights, but at the time I could only wonder if this type of activity would be covered by the company's employee compensation plan in the event the challenger prevailed.

As with all the other of his athletic pursuits, John is an avid skier. There are many modifications of ski equipment designed for physically challenged individuals, like blind skiers and those with no legs. For someone with two good legs, however, there are almost no adaptations needed, except for a way to hold a pole. John had a ski hand designed and began to challenge the moguls, first in Colorado and then in Utah. When he skied in Vail in the 1970's he was wearing his hook at the ticket booth when the attendant, citing the commitment Colorado ski resorts had made to disabled skiers, informed him he could ski as often as he wanted for no charge. Several fellow skiers in line behind him briefly considered self-amputation as they envied his entitlement.

The ski hand is a combination of the useful and the esthetic—a strapless modified artificial forearm complete with a flesh-toned fist that is permanently attached to the ski pole. Of course, there is no need for a ski glove on an artificial hand, so the ski hand remains pink in all weather conditions. While zooming down a run in Utah, John took a fall and became separated from the hand and pole, which remained standing upright in the snow underneath a ski lift while John and the rest of his equipment tumbled some 100 yards further down the hill.

Horrified lift-riders called the ski patrol in droves to report a newly-disarmed skier.

The Golf Years

A golf joke that often makes the rounds goes something like this:

A male foursome is on the sixteenth hole of a local golf course, near a road that passes by one of the fairways. Joe is getting ready to putt, when he looks up and notices a funeral procession driving slowly by. He drops his putter, removes his hat, and places his hand solemnly over his heart, remaining in this position until the hearse and other cars are well out of sight. As Joe picks up his putter and resumes his stance, one of his fellow players remarks, "That was really impressive to watch you show such respect." Joe answers, "Well, it was the least I could do for Sue. We just had our forty-ninth wedding anniversary. She was the best wife a man could have wanted."

After years of grumbling about golf having been the other woman in our relationship, I found myself falling in love with it in the 1990's, so I *get* the universal irony of this humorous story.

Many people these days write Advance Directives for family members and health care providers relative to their wishes at the end of life. It truly makes things easier for the ones left behind if the passing person can exercise some direction in these matters. My Advance

Directive for John, witnessed by several of my girlfriends and agreed to by him, reads, "Should I pass away while John is playing golf he is not to be notified until he finishes the first nine holes, or the last nine if my death occurs after he has made the turn. In the case of his playing in a tournament, if he is in a position to win, he is not to be notified until the end of regulation, unless he is in a playoff, in which case the news is to be kept from him until after the playoff has ended. Once he has been notified, he shall engage in three days of grief for the loss of his wife—his right hand—since he spent two days grieving the loss of his left hand."

Recently we had the opportunity to do a test-run on this agreement. I had just finished playing in the Senior Women's Club Championship at our home course and was riding in a cart with my playing partner to the parking lot to unload our clubs in to our cars before attending the awards luncheon. On our way to the lot, we passed John who was walking to the first tee box to start play in a scramble outing for his men's club. I wished him luck and told him I had played—or failed to play—myself completely out of competition, which was not unusual for a golfer of my caliber.

We unloaded my partner's clubs into her new white Jaguar. A loose ball fell out of her bag and began rolling down the slight hill next to the parked cars. She motioned me to go ahead with the cart to my car while she chased after the ball. I removed my clubs from the back of the cart, placing them in the floor of the passenger side and started on around the back of the cart for the driver's side. Before I could re-enter the cart on the driver's side, the golf bag took a leftward roll, landing on the forward petal and pinning it to the floor. The driverless cart lurched forward in an arc, heading first towards the back end of an Escalade, then towards the white Jaguar, with me fervently asking God to please not let it hit the Jag. Prayers answered, it turned further, hitting me and knocking me down, breaking my ribs in the process, before then plowing in to the back of a Lexus.

As the ambulance crew arrived and began to load me on to a stretcher for transport to a hospital, someone asked if they should notify John. I replied that our agreement did not spell out what was to happen in the event I was seriously ill or injured but had not died while he was playing golf, so I would prefer to not tell him. When it became apparent I would need someone to sign papers at the hospital and I was not thought to be in condition to do so, I reluctantly agreed for the club pro to go get him.

By then John was on the first green and when told his wife was being loaded in to an ambulance, he said, "Oh no. I was just getting ready to putt for birdie."

He sank the putt.

I have not been on the scene when most of the golf stories about John's arm have happened so most of them have been told to me by his buddies, usually accompanied by so much laughter they can barely get the words out of their mouth for choking on their tears. Recently his golfing friend, Bill H remembered the one about when the two of them were sitting in the Grill Room after a round. John had removed his prosthesis after the eighteenth hole and left it outside in his golf bag. He was sitting at the table with an Arnie Palmer in his right hand. His stump was resting on the edge of the table, holding down a stash of one dollar bills he had just won.

A boy of about nine, who had been on the practice range with his father, was seated at a table near enough to John for him to see the stump. He had been staring at it for several minutes when John noticed his gaze and turned to the boy, saying, "Son, golf is a dangerous game. A person can lose an arm or a leg if you're not careful."

The boy's eyes popped open, and without uttering a word, he stood and walked backwards out of the dining room.

If John's game has not gone well on a particular day, he cannot rest until he figures out what has gone wrong. Rather than join the group for a little refreshment after such a round, he goes to the range, where he practices relentlessly, hitting bucket after bucket of balls, often when others have gone home or the weather has become almost unplayable.

One afternoon in late spring, he had practiced until the threatening rain had become a reality and only one other golfer, his friend Jim, remained on the range. As thunder and lightning approached, the golf shop sounded the warning horn, forcing John to give up on practice. He took off his golf hand, laying it on the ground next to his clubs, and replaced it with the hook prosthesis, then hurriedly packed his gear and headed towards the parking lot, tipping the bill of his cap to Jim, who was also loading his equipment. A few minutes after arriving home, the phone rang.

"Hell, John, don't you even know when to bring that damn artificial arm in out of the rain?" boomed Jim's voice. "I've left it in the pro shop to dry out and you can get it next time when you come to the club."

Every week since about 2005 John has played cards with a group of men. Among the regulars are Jim, Dave, Doc, John, and Bill. They meet in the basement of Bill's home, a large open-plan house with soaring ceilings and rooms that flow from one into another. John likes to get there early so he can have the best choice of seats at the table. Dave and Jim are less picky about their seats. Doc almost always gets there just at the last minute and takes whatever seat is left.

In order to hold a handful of cards John needs to wear his hook, which is known to this group as his card playing hand. One night he was running late and he left home without putting on his card playing hand. As with most groups there are rules of order, and one of their rules is that if a player is not in his seat when play commences he is out of the game for the night. John was feeling lucky that night and did not want to miss an opportunity to fleece a few of his buddies, so he explained the situation to the others and opted to stay and to play with his myoelectric hand instead of his card-playing hand.

He had just picked up this particular hand from the prosthetic office a few days before. When he used it at home we noticed it was unusually noisy, making a distinct purring or whining sound when he thought it to open or close. We hosted dinner in our home during the previous weekend, and as John was pouring drinks and passing them around, one of the guests said, "I keep hearing a cat, but I don't see any evidence of one." We laughed when John told his friend that we did not have a cat and that it was his arm that was making the sound.

Doc arrived as expected just as the game was starting. He sat down with no preliminary chitchat and play started quickly. Usually Doc was pretty quiet, sitting almost unmoving and concentrating on his cards. Bill noticed something seemed different in Doc's behavior tonight—every few minutes he would look up towards the ceiling or peer over his shoulder towards the great room. After a couple of rounds of play, Doc turned to Bill and asked, completely serious, "Where are those birds? I keep hearing birds singing but I can't see them. Do you have an aviary in the next room?"

Bill replied, "I don't have any birds in here, Doc. That's John's damn artificial hand making that racket."

One of the other rules for the card group is that after each dealer has completed his round, he then shuffles the cards for the next dealer. It is pretty much impossible for a one-handed person to shuffle a deck of cards, even if he is wearing a card playing hand. Years ago when this same situation arose in family card games, my now-deceased mother gave John an electric card shuffler.

This device, about the size of a small shoebox, has two slots on either side of the top, where a deck can be manually placed, half on one side and half on the other. A push button in the center of the top engages simple gears that propel the cards a few at a time from either side into a center well, where they fall stacked to a receptacle below. After running a deck through this device several times, supposedly they will be well-mixed.

The grandchildren love everything about this machine. It whirs and grinds, things fly inside it, it stops and goes with the press of a finger, and they—whose hands and coordination are not adept at shuffling—can be full participants in a game of Go Fish or UNO from an early age.

After John brought his shuffler to the weekly card game and used it for a time or two, the other players declared they had made a new rule. John was never to shuffle again, they told him, and instead one of them would cover for him.

Many of these men have also golfed together for a number of years so they know each other pretty well, and are fairly desensitized to the hand and hook, or so they thought. A few years ago a foursome from the card players group traveled in Bill's car to a course some thirty minutes from their home turf. They were nearly late for their tee time and had to hurry to get all their equipment out of the trunk and onto their carts before they missed the cutoff time.

It always takes John a little longer than the others to get his golf stuff assembled, since he has to remove his myoelectric hand and strap on his golf prosthesis, plus he needs extra time to put on golf shoes and otherwise gear up with only one hand. Sometimes after removing his hand, he stuffs it into his golf bag and takes it on the course with him, but his more typical routine is to lock the hand in the open position, palm side up, and place it on the floor of the car's trunk right next to his regular shoes. That way, when everybody returns from a round and starts grabbing and stowing, he can locate what he needs fairly easily.

John and Jim were in one cart and Dave and Bill in another. The two carts were headed for the first tee box when Dave remembered he had left his golf glove in the now closed trunk. He and Bill retraced their route, parking the cart just behind the car. Bill punched the trunk release on his key chain, popping open the trunk just as Dave got there.

Seeing the upturned palm of a hand lying there on the floor of the trunk, Dave jumped back and began to yell, practically falling apart in fright. Hearing the commotion, John and Jim turned their cart back and followed their buddies to the parking lot, whereupon John shouted to Dave, "Hey, Dave, quit messing with my arm. You'll lose your own to me as soon as we start playing, but you can't have mine."

As often happens in golfing circles, some players seem to gravitate to each other, making frequent golfing trips together and learning pretty well each other's strengths and challenges. John, Roger, and Johnny started golfing together in the Nashville area in the late 1970's. They took to the road in the 1980's, visiting Pinehurst, Kiawah and Seabrook Islands, Callaway Gardens, and Fairfield Glade golf resorts among others. Usually they played eighteen holes every day, but occasionally they added a second round, for a total of thirty-six holes a day.

All this activity made them hungry and by the time they sat down in a restaurant in the evening they were impatient for service and for food. On one such occasion they were seated in a back corner of a relatively empty dining room in one of the above resorts, waiting it seemed to them way too long for the wait person, a young woman, to take their order. When she brought drinks to the people seated at the table next to them and ignored their hungry looks again, John removed his myoelectric hand, pushed the sensor button to open it, then holding it in his right hand, he extended his reach until the hand made contact with the server's apron, whereupon he pushed the close sensor, attaching the hand to the apron.

As the server felt the weight of some unknown object tugging at her uniform, she glanced down and saw the upturned hand clinging firmly to the hem of her apron. With a look of bewilderment on her face, she turned towards the golfers' table, whereupon Roger told her, completely with a straight face, "Honey, we could see how busy you are here tonight so we decided to give you a helping hand."

The three of them were all heavy sleepers. In some of the places they stayed there were no clocks on the bedside tables, so they needed to receive wake up phone calls from the front desk each morning. Even then, sometimes one of them would fall back asleep and need to have one of the others knock on his door lest they miss their tee time.

On this particular occasion John had placed his artificial arm, with his wrist watch in place, on the bedside table with the watch face turned where he could easily see it in the morning. Before going to sleep he had taken out his hearing aid and had slept soundly through the wake up call. When the sun's rays came through the curtains and woke him up, he was glad to see by his watch that it was only 6:30, so he went back to sleep. He awakened to insistent banging on his door, along with yelling from Roger and Johnny, telling him they were due on the tee box in thirty minutes. He picked up his hand, seeing the watch still said it was 6:30, and made his way to the door.

"Get your clothes on. We're late," Roger instructed.

"It's only 6:30. Why are you making such a big deal?" John retorted, pointing to his watch.

"6:30 my ass—it's almost a quarter to nine. Give me that hand," Johnny commanded.

Holding the hand, Johnny put the watch to his ear, and after a few moments he declared that the watch was not running.

"That can't be," said John. "It has a motion controlled automatic winder so it will never run down."

Roger grabbed the hand and began to shake it. "Hell, John, for an automatic winder to work it has to have wrist motion. I don't think that damn artificial hand of yours has much wrist motion."

Handing the prosthesis back to John, he said, "Here, now I've shaken up your watch. Grab your clubs and let's get going."

༢

Even in the late 1990's Kiawah, an Atlantic Ocean barrier island about thirteen miles long between Hilton Head and Charleston, South Carolina, was relatively undeveloped. This area of palmetto, scrub, and not much else had been occupied mostly by Native Americans and alligators until the mid-1700's when two large rice-growing plantations were established on the island. By the early 1900's, a descendant of the rice planter began consolidating large parcels of land into single family ownership. In the 1950's, after that family had died off or moved away, Kiawah became a timber logging site, and then in 1974 the Kuwait Investment Company, foreseeing a profit in helping wealthy Americans enjoy the good life, bought the island and began to develop golf courses and expensive vacation homes. In 1976 the Marsh Point (now Cougar Point) Golf course, a Gary Player course, opened.

John's dad moved to Wadmalaw Island, near Kiawah, when he retired in 1979. Our family was among the first spectators to visit Kiawah, as the ever-curious John scouted prospective new places to enjoy playing golf. Each time our car approached the entry gate at Kiawah, which was guarded by Arabs in fatigues, we were looked over thoroughly before being given the okay to pass. As the driver for these family ventures, John usually did not place his stump or hook on the edge of the rolled-down car window. In some Muslim countries, punishment for theft or highway robbery is to cut off the criminal's hand or foot.

In the late 1980's the Kuwaitis sold the island to an American developer who lengthened the main road somewhat and soon thereafter opened the Jack Nicklaus-designed Turtle Point Course. In the early 1990's they opened what has become the most famous of Kiawah Island's five golf courses, the Pete and Alice Dye-designed Ocean Course, site of the U.S. Ryder Cup victory in 1991. The Ocean Course was followed by the Tom Fazio-designed Osprey Point, and by the residents-only Kiawah Island Course.

While the area was visited every year by many golfers and vacationers, it remained pretty empty of permanent human residents even as late as the 2000 census, when a little more than1100 people claimed residency. Until about this time, it was common for a motorist traveling along the main road or a golfer chasing a ball along one of the fairways or preparing to putt on a green to come face to face with an alligator. Nowadays the resort management captures and relocates large alligators, though smaller ones are seen frequently throughout the island.

Alligators do not get to be twelve feet long by fasting. While a gator's preferred food is fish or fowl, which they locate in freshwater by sensing splashes, they are lightning fast on land and their formidable jaws can take down a deer or human who wanders too close to water's edge. If hungry enough, alligators are known to hunt down dogs and cats and anything else edible that is within their range. When a gator is full, its favorite pleasure is to lie in the warm sun. The Kiawah alligators surely rejoiced when the developers put sandy beaches and ponds all along their habitat, even if their peaceful slumber was occasionally interrupted by yells of "fore."

The fairway of the dogleg left par five ninth hole at Turtle Point is about a half-mile inland, receiving mild to heavy breezes depending on the whims of nature. John had just hit his second shot, a three-wood with a little draw that carried about two-hundred yards in light wind, landing on the left side of the fairway beside a pond. He saw the ball take a bounce before stopping, and he felt sure he had reached a spot from where he could make an easy chip then possibly hole out for birdie.

His playing partners, Roger and Johnny, were in another cart, and while John stowed his club in his bag and re-boarded his cart, they drove on ahead to locate their respective balls. As Roger and Johnny's cart approached John's ball, they hesitated, then made a quick u-turn, and from there turned their cart into the fairway and stopped, both men remaining firmly seated while they pointed towards the location of John's ball.

Approaching the afore-spotted location, John saw there might be a problem with getting his birdie. His ball was firmly wedged between the left rear leg and body of a twelve foot slumbering alligator, the snout facing him, lying between the fairway and the pond. The ball, sparkling white in the sun, was sitting up high enough to possibly be knocked loose with just the right lob wedge, but that would require choking down on the shaft, which John cannot easily do because of his prosthesis.

Golf rules specify that if a ball in play comes to rest on a movable obstruction, the ball may be lifted and the obstruction moved. The ball must then be replaced as near as possible to the spot directly under the place where the ball lay in or on the obstruction but not nearer the hole. (ROG rule 24-1) As John eyed the now-awake gator, each player in this match discerning his next move, the gator suddenly spun, making a ninety-degree turn and heading directly for the water, carrying John's ball along with him. John took a water ball penalty stroke and finished the hole with a bogey.

On another day while playing in the same three-some on the par five eighteenth hole of the Osprey Course, John pulled his tee shot. The ball landed in marshy ground on the left side of the fairway a few feet from the edge of a pond. Golf rules permit a player to move a ball from where it is standing in casual water, but John decided he could hit from this lie, even though his feet were almost at water's edge. He pulled out a four iron, slid it into his golf prosthesis, and gripped down on the shaft as far as possible with his right hand, adjusting his stance so he could get maximum lift under the sodden ball.

As he finished the shot which landed about 150 yards further on down the fairway, the club head was covered in the muddy divot. Releasing his right hand from the club, he kept the shaft wedged in his golf-prosthesis. Pivoting to face the pond, he extended his left arm and prosthesis/four iron towards the water, immersing the club head and shaking it for good measure as the marsh mud held on tight.

A huge gator which the threesome had seen lounging beside the pond as they approached the area suddenly cannon-balled, making fast time for John's club head. Johnny and Roger covered their faces, unable to watch the enormous creature which was about to take the club and the rest of their buddy's arm for its next meal.

Peeking out to see John holding the golf club as a weapon while backing away from the pond, his golf shoes sucking with each muddy step, Roger shouted, "That damn gator's ticked off. Offer him your other hand from your bag—the one with the watch."

While playing a friendly match in about 1990 at the Shark River Golf Course, an 18-hole municipal course in Neptune, New Jersey, with his childhood friend, Lou, a normie golfer, John was one down with four holes to go. The two old friends had been joined on the first tee by a couple of normie golfers who had never met either John or Lou. Approaching the par five 522-yard fifteenth hole, Lou had the honors. He landed his tee shot in the middle of the fairway about half way to the hole.

John looked over the situation, and then he bent down to tee up his ball. Standing up again, he pulled the arm strap on his golf prosthesis and lapped it in place, ensuring a tight hold against the pull it would face as the fully loaded club powered through at the end of his swing, and then he reached into his golf bag and pulled out his driver. Holding the club loosely in his right hand, he slid the shaft of the driver in place in his prosthesis. Seeing the grip firmly seated in the adaptive piece of the universal joint, he placed the fingers of his right hand on the shaft and took his stance. After waggling the club a couple of times, he turned his head to gaze for a moment at the chosen target, about thirty yards ahead of where Lou's ball had landed. He dipped his left shoulder slightly, then rotated on his spine to the right and pulled his right arm around his right shoulder until his wrist cocked. Pausing momentarily in full wind up, he then began to pull the club through with his left upper arm, feeling extra thrust from his legs as his hand rotated to neutral then began to re-cock as the club cleared his right hip.

Just as the club face struck the ball, the strap on his prosthesis broke, sending the ball, club, and still-attached prosthesis sailing in a high arc straight down the fairway, where all parts landed about fifty yards in front of the tee box.

Knowing he would have to take a one stroke penalty for a second tee shot, he nevertheless chose that option and hurried to retrieve his flyaway parts. The golf prosthesis was done for but the club and ball were playable. As he was returning to the tee box, the other

three players conferred. Making up a special local rule
on the spot, they decided this situation warranted giving
John another shot off the tee box with no penalty
stroke. He had no back up golf arm in his bag, so he
teed up the ball, and holding the driver in his right hand
only, he powered the ball to a pristine spot of grass just
past where Lou's ball was waiting. Lou made bogey and
John holed out in four more strokes and was all square
with three holes to go.

John learned from this experience, and thereafter
he carried in his bag a back up golf hand to use in case
the primary one broke. He was playing in the final
round of the Michigan Amputee Tournament at the
Pine View Golf Course in Three Rivers when it
happened again. He reached into his bag, withdrew the
spare, strapped it on, and holed out on his way to
winning the arm division of that tournament in 1992.

In a different variation on the theme of his golf
prosthesis breaking during mid-swing, there is the
story that while playing with Doc on their home
course, John's ball was lying up in the par five fairway
after his drive. He chose a three-wood and locked it in
place in his golf hand. As he made a full rotation in his
backswing and was just starting his downswing, the
pin in the universal joint slipped and the tapered
adapter came off, causing the golf prosthesis to hit him
in the back of the head. Doc, a retired US Army

colonel and the former head of orthopedics at a large medical center, is not easily ruffled. Determining John was not bleeding and was still functional, Doc said, "Well, since that was only your takeaway and you had not really engaged in your down stroke, I'll only make you take a half stroke penalty to replay the shot."

On another occasion just before John's seventieth birthday, he was playing what he described later as the worst round of golf in his life—enough that he was thinking about giving up the sport. Lying one in the fairway of the par-five seventeenth hole, about 180 yards from the green, he chose his 7-wood and pulled the shaft through his prosthesis, then lined up and struck the ball. He says he knew it was a pretty good shot, but not until the other players in his foursome approached the green and discovered his ball in the hole, did he find he had just made an extremely rare double eagle—sometimes called an albatross.

"Guess I'll play a few more rounds," he said.

Among the many places John has enjoyed golfing with the NAGA, perhaps none is more a favorite return venue for him than the Brickyard Crossing Course that adjoins the Indianapolis Motor Speedway. Initially there was a nine-hole course independent of Brickyard Crossing within the Speedway. When Brickyard Crossing was re-configured in the 1990's, the short course was removed, but four of the nine holes within the Speedway were incorporated into the present Brickyard Crossing course. On days when the racers are practicing or there are demo races taking place, the overpowering smell of burnt rubber can almost take away one's breath when playing these four holes.

If John had not aspired to be a jet pilot he might have chosen to become a race driver. He can barely stand to ride in a car unless he is the driver and on many occasions, friends who have been passengers in the car cockpit with him have remarked at how fast he drives, some refusing to ever repeat that error in judgment. It is not far from the truth that he files a flight plan before takeoff even if he is only carrying a load of garbage in our little pickup truck taking it to the county landfill down the road from us.

When he was in his late forties he bought the car of his inner sixteen-year-old's dreams—a turbo-charged 1990 Ford Thunderbird, which could do 120 mph with practically no effort and with a top speed of 155 mph. It was one of his great sorrows when a couple of years later our then college-aged son fell asleep at the wheel of that car and plowed it between two trees in the woods near where we live, demolishing the vehicle. When son Jon phoned us at 4:00 AM to tell us first that he was unhurt and second the car would never again be driven, I am not sure I know which was the greater of John's tears—sadness for the loss of the car or gratitude for the life of our son which that Thunderbird's sturdy steel body had saved.

While John never got to qualify as a civilian race driver at the Indy 500 track, he did compete as a formula one driver at Myrtle Beach. The Strand at Myrtle Beach has a greater concentration of public access golf courses in its thirty mile span than does anyplace else in the world. This was just exactly what he and another group of men, including Corbin, an amp whose leg was blown off by a mine while he was serving as a US Army chaplain in Vietnam, and Jack, a fellow clergyman and normie, along with five other guys including two who had grown up in Indianapolis and attended Speedway High School and had not missed a 500 race since age twelve, found attractive about this oceanside resort.

John and Corbin have played together for more than twenty-five years on the NAGA circuit—long enough for Corbin to know John's moves pretty well. While other golfers, including some well-known professionals curse and swear at bad shots, John's routine response to a shot he has poorly hit is to yell, "Oh no!" Over the years Corbin has heard so many utterances of "oh no" that he no longer calls him John, substituting instead the nickname of Oh No. Christmas cards sent to us from Corbin are usually addressed to Mr. and Mrs. Oh No.

At Myrtle Beach the marathon-loving golfers could easily play two complete rounds of golf—thirty-six holes—each day for a week and still have a little time left over in the evening to pursue the local attractions. One of those attractions was a Formula One racing experience at a local raceway, where amateur drivers could compete on a course against an actual time set by a professional racer. By the time John's golfing group got to the park, it was late in the day and quite a few amateur racers had already established their best times. John took a look at what he determined to be their minimally acceptable times, then bought a ticket and suited up for his three laps in an actual race car on the professional course. While Corbin and Jack offered prayers to whatever gods could protect such a daredevil, John breezed through the laps with the best time of the day.

As John came off the race track, certificate of accomplishment in hand, Corbin asked, "I wonder what Mrs. Oh No will say about this?"

John grew up fishing in the Atlantic Ocean. Before his accident it was nothing to him to bait a hook, reel in a catch, then pull the fishhook out of the mouth and throw the struggling fish back in the water to swim again. There are not any oceans near where we have lived in Nevada or Tennessee but there is plenty of fresh water fishing, and it seems the routine is the same wherever there is man and fish.

Sometimes if a fish takes a hook in the corner of its mouth, it is relatively easy to get the hook out and to release the fish. If the fish takes the hook all the way through the lower part of its jaw, however, it is much more difficult to get it out without harming the fish.

Usually a specially adapted needle nose pliers is required to do this job, and even then, when a slippery fish is desperate to get away, the job is easier said than done.

In the late 1970's John fished with Johnny and his dad, Charlie, from their boat above Old Hickory Dam and in Priest Lake and other places wherever the fish were biting in Middle Tennessee. Charlie had never seen John's hook trick until one day when they were catching so fast they could hardly get a breath. As the stripes practically jumped into the boat, John would hold the squirming, slippery fish tightly in his right hand and grip the mouth hook with his prosthetic hook and gently work it out, while Charlie watched gaping.

"It's good to have a hook," John told him with a wink, to gales of laughter from all three men.

Fly fishing while wearing a hook is much more technically difficult than is fishing using a rod and reel. John says it literally is like doing the process with one arm tied behind the back. The hooks are tiny; the line is enormously long; the flies are literally tied onto the fish hook. Most fly fishing takes place from either the banks or the bed of a stream, usually a very fast running one, which frequently has rocks covered in mossy slime.

While on a return trip to Nevada a few years ago, John and Cliff were joined by another John, and a guide. They took their horses high in the Rubies and fished in pristine alpine lakes, catching brookies and rainbows all day long. They kept only enough fish for their dinner and were eager to chow down once the day's catch was over. As they began to build the cook fire, the fishermen realized they had forgotten to pack cooking utensils.

"It's no problem, guys," John told them. "I have a built-in implement."

He placed the several whole trout in the hot grease in the frying pan with expertise, delicately reaching in just as the fish began to flake and flipping each trout to the other side. When all were done, he lifted each browned and sizzling fish from the grease and placed it on the plates, then removed the pan, holding the hot skillet handle with his prosthetic hook. As the coals began to dim, he reached deep under them with his hook and gave them a good turn, readying the fire for the after dinner coffee pot.

"It's good to have a hook," he said. The diners nodded in appreciation.

On a fishing adventure to the Green River in southwest Wyoming with our then thirty-something-year-old son, Jon, the two men kept in touch with walkie-talkies. Son Jon is an expert fly fisherman, casting with grace and skill, and almost never spooking the catch as he perfectly lays out the line. Dad John sometimes struggles a little, both with the skills of tying on the fly and with the art of the figure eight windup and the stiff wristed release of the leader. Nevertheless, both men were catching quickly on this late fall day. The cold clear water rushed downstream, causing little eddies which were good targets for the largest trout. Occasional snowflakes told them winter would soon be there so they needed to get their quotas in the creel early on.

The elder John worked his way up river and out of sight of the younger Jon. Just before lunch he touched base to say he was having little luck from the shallow edges so thought he would wade further out in the stream. He stowed the walkie-talkies in his jacket on the bank and trudged to the center of the river. His chest high waders were heavy, but he was glad he had worn them as his feet slipped a little on the mucky slick rocks underfoot. Suddenly his feet flew out from under him and he was caught in the rushing water, being hurled downstream. His waders began to take on water and he struggled to try to right himself, to no avail. Not wanting to lose his expensive fly rod, he clutched it in his right hand as he was propelled towards where Jon was fishing.

Jon could hear his dad yelling before he could actually see him. Suddenly he saw upturned boots and a hand holding a fly rod coming at him in the middle of the river. He could do nothing to stop the virtual raft as it sped by, so he exited the water quickly and began to work his way down the river's edge. About fifty feet farther downstream Jon saw his dad's prosthetic hook hanging onto an overhanging scrub tree. As he got closer, he could see the hook was still attached to his dad, who was being buffeted by the rushing water virtually unable to do anything but wait for help. Jon could reach enough over the lifesaving tree to take the fly rod from his dad's hand, freeing the hand to be used to pull himself, hand over hook, closer to the shore. With Jon's help, John could then pull himself, soaked to the skin and freezing but alive, out of the river.

When he could get his breath, he whispered, "It's good to have a hook." Son Jon smiled.

What do you say if you meet an amp on the road?

When John and I attend normie golf social functions together there are almost always men and women in attendance whom I have met before. Invariably John is recognized immediately, while folks usually cannot place me unless I am standing with him. He asked me recently why I thought that happens.

"Because there are just not too many one-armed golfers like you out there," I said. "And also because you have really good looking legs and you wear shorts almost all year round."

In social interactions with John and his hand or hook, initially people either do not realize he is an amputee and then seem embarrassed when they do realize it, or they just try to ignore the hand all together. If he is wearing a coat and tie, it can be difficult at first to notice the hand, but if he is in short sleeves the hand or hook cannot be easily overlooked.

We were visiting friends in Florida and were dressed casually for the season. A woman we had never met dropped by with her husband for lunch, and upon meeting John and noticing his somewhat different forearm and hand, she seemed not to register that it was artificial. Trying to be solicitous, she asked him, "Do you have tennis elbow?" then, realizing her faux pas, she turned away and never spoke to him again during lunch or afterwards.

At a formal affair attended by several couples, John was seated at the dining table next to Dianne, whom he had never met, the very attractive girlfriend of his golfing buddy, Roger. Roger, who knew John was completely open about his situation, decided to play a practical joke on Dianne by telling her that John was very sensitive about his handicap and no matter what she might feel like doing or saying during dinner, she absolutely must not acknowledge John's hand and was to avoid looking at it or making any comments about it.

Even in a formal setting where the plates are served and removed by wait staff, diners still pass bread and butter and condiments to their fellow tablemates either at their left or at their right. Dianne was on John's left side, and he was in on the joke. Remaining completely serious, he regularly picked up the butter, salt, bread basket, and pepper shaker with his prosthesis, a move which is hard to ignore because it looks somewhat awkward as he uses an exaggerated lifting motion of his prosthetic hand as he hovers then grasps an item. Additionally, the artificial hand sometimes does not release immediately when he thinks it to release, or in this case, when he withheld the thought. As he passed item after item to Dianne, the hand would stay firmly attached to whatever he was passing no matter how hard she tugged. By the end of dinner, when Roger and John let Dianne in on the joke, she was almost a nervous wreck with trying to balance being polite and uninterested while at the same time being considerate and kind. Luckily, Dianne, who eventually married Roger, was a good sport and has remained a good friend but twenty-five years after this happened, she shakes her finger at John and laughs about her introduction to the hand.

John's brother, Dick, re-married in 1996 in a garden setting outside Philadelphia. John was the best man, a role he carried out with appropriate solemnity as the wedding partners exchanged their vows in a gazebo, surrounded by fifty or so family and friends. As the wedding photos were being snapped afterwards, the photographer instructed John to put his hand on his brother's shoulder. With no change in demeanor, John quickly unbuttoned his shirt cuff and reached up the left sleeve and withdrew his prosthesis, placing it deftly on his brother's left shoulder, then backing away. The photographer gasped and stopped taking pictures for awhile, while John and Dick dissolved in laughter. Thirteen years later, as John prepared to be best man at our son's beachside wedding the two brothers recreated the scene for another photographer, who this time was forewarned.

Children are fascinated by both the hook and the hand and often stare openly or sometimes approach him to ask a question. Repeatedly we notice their parents trying to shush them or redirect their interest, with all the best intentions of being socially correct or at least not being intrusive, but sometimes it seems as if they are saying, "Maybe he doesn't know he is an amputee and we mustn't tell him the secret."

**John and Dick re-enacting hand on shoulder scene
at Jon's wedding. 2009**

Years ago, when we visited overnight in the home of our friends, Dave, a pediatrician, and Betsy, a medical social worker, John sat down at their piano and started to play, whereupon their five-year old daughter, Karyn, retreated to her room. Emerging soon, she carried with her a book with black and white photographs of persons with various disabilities engaging in activities just as normies do. Karyn opened the book to a picture depicting an arm amputee and showed it to John. Not realizing that she was trying to communicate with him her compassion about his situation, something her parents had been coaching her about, John looked at her and asked, "Do you think I have a disability?" Karyn closed the book and fled the room in tears.

John learned from this experience and nowadays whenever a child approaches him in wonder, he answers honestly about his missing limb and often invites the child, and any others, to visit with him and to touch and feel the prosthesis. They are usually amazed when they learn they can make the hand open and close themselves by touching the sensors on the inside of the casing.

While growing up, our own children provided numerous school teachers opportunity to sensitize students to disabilities when they brought their dad's hook and hand—and occasionally his ear—to Show and Tell. Our oldest grandson, Grant, who spent a good bit of time with us when he was just learning to talk, could speak clearly at a young age. When he was barely older than two and accompanied us on an outing, like to a mall or the grocery store, he would regularly approach total strangers and say, "My granddaddy can take his hand off." Since there was little mistaking what he had just said, the reactions were first to puzzle that they had heard him correctly and then to politely say, "Oh, that's nice," while discreetly moving away from Grant and trying to not be obvious as they looked his grandfather over.

Sometimes the hand has a mind of its own. John often removes the prosthesis when he comes into the house, placing it on whatever portion of the counter top in our kitchen may be open. Once, as we were starting to eat dinner, we heard the unattached hand start opening and closing, something we came to attribute to our long-dead last pet, Murdoch, who now gets blamed for most anything that is missing or acts up.

Every holiday offers an opportunity for a hand-related event. Once John volunteered to play Santa for the children's nursery school, and that night numerous children told their parents that they had not previously known that Santa wore a hook. And then there is Halloween, when John always answers the doorbell clutching a bag of candy in the prongs of his hook to which apparition the visiting ghosts and goblins shout, "Oh, man, that's a really neat Captain Hook costume."

Annually since 2004 we have traveled to Puerto Vallarta, commonly called PV, a lovely Pacific coastal town of about 150,000 folks directly west of Guadalajara, the capital of Jalisco, Mexico, where we spend the Thanksgiving holiday far from North American turkey and dressing. The weather in PV is great this time of year and we have been delighted by the setting and the staff at the Marriott Resort where we stay.

John's routine is to get out early in the morning and place several towels on his favorite recliners to claim our poolside seating underneath two huge palm trees. After a leisurely breakfast, he is ensconced on his chair for the rest of the day, surveying the beach vendors who are setting up shop, and generally doing little else. As the day warms up, he frequently cools off in the pool, slipping his prosthesis off and placing it on the recliner next to the stack of *National Geographic* magazines that he brings along to read each year.

The first time he left his arm there to guard his turf, I wondered if this was such a good idea, since we did not really know anyone else who might come by. Maybe someone would want to take his arm home as a souvenir. Maybe the arm might get displaced and without any identifying information he would not be able to find it.

I need not have worried. We had barely gotten into our room that first visit when John turned to me, a pained look on his face, and announced that his arm was broken. He had picked up a new arm from his prosthetician a day or so before we departed for our vacation and he had worn the arm on the plane for the first time. In the process of carrying his luggage, somehow the screw that holds in place the battery casing had become dislodged and had fallen out, causing the electrodes in the inside of the prosthesis to fail to connect with the sensitive areas on his stump.

John giving a wave from his perch poolside in PV 2011

Picking up the hotel telephone, he called the operator, telling her in her own language, that he was a newly arrived hotel guest and that his arm was broken. In response to the operator's question about sending a doctor, John said, "No, gracias. Please just call the maintenance crew and ask them to come to my room and bring some Allen wrenches, screwdrivers, and an assortment of screws."

Within ten minutes, the maintenance crew leader and an assistant knocked on our door and were admitted, carrying a large tool case and trying to not appear too overly concerned about the reported broken arm, while at the same time inquiring how they might be of assistance. John picked up his prosthesis from where he had placed it on the desk, turning it over to show them where the screw was missing and asked them to help him find the right replacement piece from their toolkit and also to tighten another piece with a wrench. The two maintenance men began speaking rapid-fire Spanish to each other. One of the men wiped his brow in relief while the other crossed himself, and then they began to search frantically in their toolbox for some part that might help mend the limb. Finding none, they assured John they would go back to their work quarters and make a better search and return shortly.

As promised, they were back in about fifteen minutes, apologizing profusely that they did not have the correct screw or wrench, but offering the universal solution for the problem—a roll of duct tape. The loose casing was quickly eased in place and securely bound and they left the duct tape behind in case we needed any more surgical tape during our visit. I am pretty sure the entire hotel staff was alerted within the hour that among their guests was a gringo speaking a little Spanish whose artificial arm might glint in the sun when the rays hit the metallic tape.

It did not take long for John and his arm to also be noticed poolside, with both adults and children curious about this one-armed man who seemed completely at ease with curiosity seekers asking questions and who actually poked fun at himself, making it vastly more easy for our new friends to also make good-natured jibes.

On a recent vacation there, Paul, one of our poolside friends, announced he was going to make a small video of the group in the pool singing Happy Birthday to his dog back home, which was lonely for her humans. "Everybody raise both hands and wave at Snickers," Paul announced as he pointed the camera at the partially submerged assembly of folks.

"I'm trying, Paul, but I'll have to get out of the pool to get my other hand if you want us to wave with two hands in the air," answered John, as the video camera rolled.

By the time the shoot was done, it was Happy Hour, and I joined John in the pool. He was holding a Negra Modelo, his drink of choice in PV, in his good hand, visiting with our new best buddies from Iowa, Texas, Indiana, Washington, and elsewhere, regular visitors like us to PV. From time to time he would use his stump to push up the bill of his cap or slide his sunglasses back up on the left side of his head.

A young friend in the group, also named John (John R), who had been in the recent movie, was by then walking through the chest deep water from the pool-center bar, a Margarita in each hand, to where his wife was waiting with the group near water's edge. First sipping on the cool drink, the younger John then looked at the older one, and asked, "So, John, back home in Tennessee what do you call the place where you keep all your artificial arms? An armory?"

On another of our November visits to PV, Brian, the younger brother of John R, who was bicycling from California to Guatemala with a friend, stopped over at the hotel for a night in a decent bed while all of us were enjoying our Thanksgiving holiday. Chilling in the pool with the group, he recounted their trip so far, which had not involved any encounters with peril, but he acknowledged that the most dangerous portion of the travels was still ahead, as they trekked towards the southern border of Mexico. John M, who monitors closely the unstable situation of internal Mexican warfare, commented to Brian, "I hope you are well-armed for this part of the trip." Without batting an eye, Brian quipped back, "I'm certainly better armed than you are." John M high-fived him with his right hand.

On our most recent PV vacation, John made it there but his arm did not. In early fall 2013 he ordered a new arm to replace the one he had been wearing for several years. The order went in to the VA during the recent government shutdown, and as happened with everything else connected to the feds during this time, the process was delayed. Three days before we were to depart for Mexico, John received notice that his new hand would be delivered to the prosthetics office on November 21—the day of our planned departure. Since our plane was to leave at about sunrise, there would be no opportunity to retrieve the new arm before we left. Hoping to make the best of it, we boarded in Nashville with John wearing his old arm and flew easily to Jalisco. By the time we arrived at our hotel, however, John was complaining loudly about the performance—or lack thereof—of the arm he was wearing. It wouldn't open, then wouldn't close, then the casing cracked and finally by the time we reached our beach chairs John had reached his limit of patience with his worthless prosthesis.

It was Friday afternoon, about 3:00, when he placed the phone call to Nashville instructing the prosthetics office to ship his new arm to him at the hotel via 2nd day air. "Insure it for $4,000," he said. They told him they had never shipped out of country before, but since it was so urgent they would get right on it. Sure enough, in a couple of hours we received a confirmatory e-mail saying the new limb had been sent by UPS Overseas Express and would be in our hotel on Monday.

Monday came and went without receipt of the arm and John began to track the shipment online. "Arrived in Mexico City, 2PM, Sunday November 24," the message in Spanish said. No delivery on

Tuesday prompted more inquiries, now with the help of the Spanish-speaking hotel concierge, Simon, a native of Great Britain.

"They tell me your arm is in customs in Guadalajara, sir. They need you to pay 40% duty—20,000 pesos—that would be USD $1600— to have it shipped here. I have my brother-in-law who works for the Mexican federal government looking into it," Simon told us.

Wednesday arrived. "Sir, I know you don't want to pay the $1600. They say if you can produce a statement from a doctor in Mexico saying why you need this equipment, maybe then they can release it to you."

Thursday— "Sir, I have just learned your arm is not really in Guadalajara. It is actually in Mexico City."

Friday— "Sir, because it is Thanksgiving weekend in the U.S., we cannot get in touch with anyone in the international division of UPS to arrange to have it shipped back to Nashville as you want."

Monday— "Sir, here are the forms for you to complete to authorize sending the arm back to the States. It will cost you another $237 to send it back."

Thursday— "We have your arm back from Mexico. You can pick it up as soon as you are back in town."

That damn artificial arm was in great shape for all its international adventures but there was not even a T-shirt to show for its vacation time.

৶

In some cases prostheses may be potential weapons and their use is sanctioned. Terror suspect, the Egyptian Islamic cleric Mustafa Kamel Mustafa, who lost both arms fighting the Soviets in Afghanistan in the 1980's and who is jailed in New York's Metropolitan Correctional Center, is not allowed to wear his prosthetic hooks most of the time because they are considered to be weapons. More than one inmate has committed further crimes while incarcerated using their prostheses to viciously attack fellow inmates or custodians.

TSA agents are appropriately curious when John's prosthesis appears in their line of sight. A few years ago John was passing through the security line in the Philadelphia airport, when a TSA agent narrowed her eyes, pointed at him, and said—almost shouted—"You're the one, aren't you? I remember you."

More than eight years before he had traveled through this same airport wearing his prosthetic hand. At that time a passenger simply walked through a metal body scanner. There were no x-ray devices with rolling belts running through them where everyone's hand luggage, computers, pocket change, shoes, and whatever else gets scanned, like today.

John knew from experience his arm would give off a signal because of the metal. Despite the fact that at the time he was in his early sixties and had an MBA and a law degree, there is an impish part of him that remains about sixteen-years-old. That juvenile part of his personality unbuttoned and reached under the cuff of his long-sleeved shirt, pulled off the hand with one movement, then handed the arm, fingers-first, across the barrier to the unsuspecting security agent, who almost passed out at receiving a life-like hand complete with fingernails and adorned with a high-end college-symbol wrist watch.

Passing through the same airport security line now, he removed the arm and placed it in one of the plastic crates located strategically at the head of the long table leading to the rolling belt and x-ray machine. He stepped through the scanning device and emerged without having set off any alarms, then faced the woman.

"Yes, maam, I'm the one," he acknowledged, smiling at her as she ID'd John to her colleagues.

"I'm glad to see you again," he said, hoping she would not have him arrested.

"I'll never forget you," she said, chuckling. As he moved out of the security area, he looked back. She was shaking her head and smiling, her eyes rolling as she recalled the scene.

On another trip out of Philadelphia, when I had accompanied him to the wedding of his brother the night before, I was in great pain. I was waiting for my first knee replacement and I wore a full leg hinged knee brace which allowed me a little more mobility than I had with an unsupported joint. Even so, it was difficult for me to stand or even to sit without discomfort and especially I hurt if I had to keep my knee bent, like in a cramped airplane row. John was solicitous and he approached the agent's podium to request a seat for both of us in the exit row, where there is much more leg room. He was wearing the navy blazer he had worn the night before at the wedding and I had on long trousers, so neither of our infirmities was evident to the cursory view of the agent, who smiled and handed him a corrected seating assignment.

Because of the bulkiness of John's prosthesis and the way it extends over the side of the arm rest, he always tries to sit in the first seat in the row on the left side of the aisle as he walks from the front of the plane. On the occasion when he has been seated elsewhere, his prosthesis has frequently jabbed the seat neighbor on his left. Arriving at our row of seats, John removed his jacket and placed it in the overhead compartment along with our carry-on luggage, then sat down, his short sleeved shirt revealing his arm prosthesis as it sat on the aisle arm rest and protruded slightly into the space above the aisle.

The flight attendant approached us and without mentioning a reason, suggested we might like to move to a seat a few rows up front of the exit row. John smiled and politely turned her down. Shortly, a second attendant approached and made a similar offer, suggesting she could also convey our stowed luggage to the new seat. Again John turned down the offer and he began to absorb himself in the reading material he always brings on board. Finally a third attendant, obviously the senior crew member, came alongside and said, "The captain has asked me to offer you and your wife a seat in first class and you can have all the drinks you'd like from here to Nashville."

John grinned and told her we would be pleased to accept their kind offer.

I have never met a one-armed paper hanger, but I have some idea about how difficult it would be for a one-armed person to hang paper—or to do quite a few things, actually. For John, it's sometimes just the opposite—having one artificial hand can occasionally be a workplace advantage.

While working as a store detective in Marshall Field's he did not always wear a weapon, relying instead on his brains and occasionally his brawn to outdo the shoplifters who made up his cases. On one occasion, he spotted two burly men riding the descending escalator to the ground floor area of the posh downtown Chicago store, carrying stuffed shopping bags in each hand. They spotted John and dropped the bags and John gave chase, accosting one of them and hurling him towards a plate glass window. His artificial arm struck the window before the criminal's body did, shattering the glass, some of which fell into John's hair and clothing. The suspect fled through the open window, and John gave chase, wrestling him to the ground and holding him pinned facedown at the neck under his prosthetic arm and hand until a Chicago police officer arrived to make the arrest.

During John's stint as a taxicab driver in Reno, all kinds of folks hitched rides. One night an especially inebriated man hailed his cab saying he wanted to go to a casino in Sparks, another town near Reno. Upon entering the cab, the man exploded in a string of expletives and cursing which continued unabated. A block or two later, John pulled over, stopped the cab and got out. He reached into the back seat, grabbing the drunk by the back of the neck with the claws of his hook, and sailed him in to the ditch that ran alongside the roadway.

In his role representing his company in labor contract negotiations with the local United Steelworkers of America union, John would usually start off the negotiations dressed in business attire wearing his prosthetic hand. Coming to terms on labor agreements is a complex event with behind the scenes as well as front and center plays. While the private talks are generally fairly affable, the public theatre is usually distinguished by dramas performed by both sides.

As hours morphed into days and no settlement was reached, John changed into battle gear wearing his hook, to which he attached three extra-wide rubber bands for additional resistance strength. As things heated up he displayed the hook prominently on the table as he sat across from the union representatives, periodically using it to pick up from the tabletop little pieces of lint or an empty drinking cup or can, sometimes managing to crush between the prongs whatever he had picked up. When negotiations dragged on for days without an agreement being reached, John eventually pounded the table with the hook, then looking the other side directly in the eyes he said, "Fellows, first you want to take the shirt off the company's backs, then the food out of our mouths, now you want me to give you the only hand I have to spare. Let's get this over now." Usually it did not take long for a conclusion to be reached once the hook took center stage.

In 1998, at age fifty-seven, after twenty-one years with the company and a plan that up until then had included working for them until he was in his late sixties, he was notified that the IKG division of Harsco was to be merged and he had three weeks until retirement. At first it seemed to him like a relief—he could play more golf—but there were bills to pay and a lifestyle to support and those realities meant it was time for him to again retrain for a new career.

He completed a course in judicial mediation and became an administrative law judge and arbitrator, working as an independent provider for several agencies, among them the New York Stock Exchange (NYSE), now Financial Industries National Review Administration (FINRA); the Securities and Exchange

Commission (SEC); the American Arbitration Association (AAA); and TENNCARE, our state's version of Medicaid. In these roles he usually works out of his home office, but when settlements cannot be reached by long-distance he travels to other locales and conducts a hearing.

Frequently these cases take place in a conference room of a hotel or in the office of one of the neutral attorneys, but occasionally they are scheduled to be heard in an actual court room, in which case he sits on the judge's bench above the participants. He does not wear judge's robes, instead wearing a suit and tie. In a recent case taking place in the courthouse in Tupelo, MS, he noticed that all the parties kept turning their heads to look up towards the bench, then gazing around in its vicinity, seemingly trying to locate the cause for a sound they kept hearing. Finally, noticing their quizzical glances, John looked down at them, smiling, and said, "Oh, it looks like you're wondering what you're hearing. I don't have a cat or a bird stashed under the bench. That sound you're hearing is coming from my artificial hand." Despite the formality of the setting and the seriousness of the proceedings, everyone laughed and the case continued with the hand occasionally purring away as Judge John moved around papers on his desk.

John's mediation training, under the Tennessee Supreme Court Rule Thirty-one, took place in Knoxville, with about thirty students in attendance. As a part of the experience the students conducted a moot mediation, where some students role-played two parties on opposite sides of a question while another student role-played the mediator whose job was to help bring agreement between the two sides. Usually this process is a little tedious and requires patience on the part of the mediator to help the parties keep the ball in play. It helps if the mediator remains composed.

Because the practice session was set up to be as close as possible to real life, the students wore business attire for the session. As usual with business wear, John wore his prosthetic hand with his suit coat. When it was his turn to be the mediator, he worked hard to bring accord between the opposing factions, but they would not budge off their distances. Growing weary of what he perceived as gaming behavior, he suddenly slammed his hand down hard on the table that sat between the parties, shaking its four legs and terrifying the student participants. He told them he meant for them to fish or cut bait and he had little time left to coddle them.

Fifteen years later, after John had not mediated for a while and needed a credentials letter from the instructor, he called her at her office in Knoxville. He started to explain who he was and when he had taken her course, when she interrupted him, laughing as she spoke.

"I've taught hundreds of students over the years and I hardly ever remember who anyone is after they have completed the course, but I've never forgotten you. Hardly a class goes by that I don't tell the story of how you got the parties to come to agreement quickly when you slammed your prosthesis down on that table."

During a hearing in Philadelphia where he commuted each day by both train and subway from his brother's home in West Chester to downtown, John was hurrying to make a connection back to the suburb after a long day sitting in coat and tie listening to testimony. Descending from ground level into the subway station he spotted his train idling at the platform and he hurried his step to make the train. Just before he approached his intended car, the sliding doors began to close and a recorded message indicated the train was about to depart. Written prominently in both Spanish and English, and repeated on the public address system by the nameless male announcer, was a stern message for all passengers to avoid trying to halt the closing of the doors by sticking an arm or other implement into the space between the two doors. Rules have always been intended for other people as far as John is concerned, especially when he is in a hurry to get somewhere.

The doors closed tightly on his prosthetic forearm and no amount of yanking would free the limb as the train began to accelerate, at first slowly, then with more speed. John walked along the side of the train, and then began to run, his arm completely under the control of the train. About fifty yards down the track the platform ended and he was posed to do an imitation of Roadrunner hitting a wall when a conductor saw his plight and pulled the emergency brake. As John lay ten feet from the end of the platform, staring at that brick façade which surely would have taken his arm off again and maybe worse, he was grateful to instead be receiving the dressing down of the conductor who made him stay in the station to fill out paperwork and whose demeanor did not improve with time. After John finally got on another train, he realized his hearing aid was missing from his right ear, dislodged by the impact, he assumed.

The next morning as he connected through the same station, he went to the train master's office to report the missing hearing aid. He was shocked when told that someone had found the device on the platform and turned it in. The train master handed it to him and when John put it back in place it worked perfectly. The same could not be said about his suit jacket. When he returned home and showed it to me, asking if I could fix it, I took one look and knew it was destined for the trash.

Sometimes the arm takes on unintended adversarial characteristics. We had visited our friends John and Janice in their home in Nevada on numerous occasions, where John M has always been friendly with Jasmine, their English spaniel, scratching her belly and playing fetch in the yard. On this particular visit he was wearing his purring prosthesis, and as he bent to pet Jasmine, she snapped at him, leaving a small impression of her front teeth in his good arm. Her owners were horrified that the always calm pet had suddenly turned vicious. "Not to worry," John M told them. "She's hearing my arm and thinks it is a predator." He removed the suspicious body part and he and Jasmine quickly resumed their friendship.

Our grandson, Alexander, will probably always remember his grandfather for an event that happened during a bonding experience between them when he was five. While visiting us in Tennessee, Alexander helped John and me clear and load brush from our yard onto our pickup truck, then they journeyed together in the truck down the road from our home to the county waste facility to dump it into a large vat. All went well with the loading and the tying down phase of the adventure and I watched them drive out of our driveway with relief that this chore was over for the time being. Ten minutes later John and Alexander roared back into the garage, anguish on John's face and astonishment registering on Alexander's.

"Where's your cell phone?" John asked.

"Here," I said, "but why do you need it?"

"Because my phone fell out of my pocket when I heaved the limbs and I need to use yours to call mine so I can dig through and find it in the bottom of the dumpster."

Off they went and when they returned about thirty minutes later, both cell phones were intact. With admiration reflecting off his face, Alexander told me, "Granddad called his phone twenty-six times from your phone while he used his hook to plow through the dumpster. And then he reached in and picked his phone up with the hook."

Since the late 1980's we have enjoyed dancing, especially the kind of dancing with which I grew up in southern Appalachia, like square dancing and buck dancing. On the surface it might not seem that a person who has two good legs and feet but is missing a hand would have to make alterations in his activity in order to dance, but there are a few adaptations that must be made. Depending on the situation or just his particular whim at the time, John might wear either his hook or his hand to a dance. When an unsuspecting dancer gets paired with John at random in a reel lineup, she is almost always initially freaked by grabbing the metal hook or the latex-gloved artificial hand.

When I am his partner for a two-step or waltz, it has been difficult for me to know whether to hold the hook or hand in my own right hand, which would be the placement with a normie partner but which gives me no feedback about the possible next foot move as does a normal hand, or whether to put my right hand on his left shoulder so I can get body clues. We have settled on the former placement, and now he calls out anticipated changes as we glide along the dance floor. Since he cannot always judge the location of his left hand by feel, as would a normie partner, sometimes he leads us into crash mode with other dancers, especially if the dance floor is crowded. He says this works to his advantage in clearing unwanted persons from the venue.

John is an accomplished buck dancer, a kind of old-time flatfoot dancing, similar to Irish step-dancing, in which the upper arms and torso remain very still while the feet rapidly tap. In order to accomplish this stature, John places the prosthetic hand with the stump in place inside it, in his left jeans pocket and locks it in place with a touch of a sensor. On more than one occasion, his dancing vigor has caused him to become unattached from the hand, which stays nicely attached to his pocket while his escaped stump waves to the crowd.

"Will you love me still, when I'm old and grey?"

There are two unfailing truths about John. He will always be a pilot and he will always be a competitive athlete. He does not need a yearly physical exam to re-qualify as a competitive athlete, and he makes use on almost a daily basis of this privilege to play golf, or tennis, or to ski, or if nothing else, to engage in a competition with the local squirrels for access rights to the seeds in the bird feeders on our deck, him armed with an air-pellet gun and the squirrels armed only with their cunning behavior. Even so, the rodents usually win this little joust.

John armed for warfare with squirrels. 2012

Life events that require John's presence must be scheduled around his competitions. I have on more than one occasion re-worked surgery dates around his golf schedules. When his mother was approaching her last months, he told her to please not die while he was playing in a golf tournament. She transitioned in January, when snow was on the ground. Our first baby was due to be born in early April, but she decided to wait until the middle of the month to make her appearance. As John stood at my bedside in the near-north side Chicago hospital where I was in early labor, he began to pace more than I would have expected of a soon-to-be-new-father. Thinking that he might be experiencing negative recall for his months in the hospital a few years before, I asked what the matter was.

"It's the Cubs home season opener against Cincinnati. Ernie Banks and Pete Rose are playing," he answered.

Wrigley Field was less than a mile away. He phoned back to the hospital during the seventh-inning stretch to see how I was progressing.

I started losing my hearing when I was in my forties, having inherited the kind of high-frequency nerve deafness experienced by my mother, grandfather, and his mother. While I resisted getting hearing aids for several years because of vanity and budget, in 1996 I finally made an appointment with an audiologist, Dr. Sheffey, a very serious, no nonsense professional. Dr. Sheffey explained that not only did I hear through the delicate mechanisms of the inner ear, but also through the sounds caught by my outer ear and funneled down the ear canal and through the voice cues I received by focusing on the mouths of people who were speaking to me. I got it that when I cupped my hand to my ear I could always hear better and I could understand why I would sometimes tell people I needed to put my glasses on in order to better hear them.

I was thrilled to be fitted with totally-in-the-canal hearing aids that both protected my vanity and were then state-of-the-art hearing devices. As I wore the new aids initially, sounds that everyone experiences day in and day out, like birds singing and voices in a crowd, were almost overwhelming to me but gradually I acclimated. It did not take long for me to begin inserting my hearing aids first thing in the morning and removing them only just as I lay down to sleep.

John had always had exceptional hearing, even in his left ear, where the damage had almost all occurred to the outside of the ear with just some minor changes in the contour of the ear canal but no interior damage as a result of the injury. As he approached his fifties, though, his hearing began to diminish, a natural part of aging, and something he vehemently denied for several years, blaming me for mumbling so he could not hear me. While a big part of his hearing loss at first could be attributed to lack of listening, it seemed to me he could actually hear better with his left ear—his bad ear—than with his right ear—his good ear, even though he did not have a left hand to cup around nor a left outer ear to be cupped.

We finally reached a point where communication between us in our car while he was driving and I was a passenger or in a restaurant with background noise was virtually impossible unless I shouted. Eventually as other people began to notice his hearing loss he decided to get a hearing evaluation for himself. Dr. Sheffey told him he had a significant loss in his good ear and a minor loss in his bad ear. At any rate, he could not be fitted with an aid for his bad ear anyway since the canal was misshapen and since there was no outer ear over which to attach the external part of a hearing aid.

On a Friday in January he picked up his single new hearing aid and was beaming with the joy of renewed sound in his life when he arrived home. We had scheduled dinner out and as we drove to the restaurant we enjoyed unforced conversation between us, since his good ear which had been his bad ear was now good again. The renewed communication continued through our meal. It felt to me like I had my husband back and I went to sleep very happy that night.

Standing in the kitchen the next morning while I poured my coffee, I heard a cream-curdling shriek emanating from the vicinity of our bathroom. Registering in my still foggy mind that he had to be alive to have made such a sound, I picked up my coffee cup and gently made my way back through the bedroom and towards the bath, hoping I would not find him lying in a pool of blood or worse.

I saw him standing in front of his sink, a look of horror on his face. Following his gaze down his left side, I saw his hook clenched tightly around a small object, with wires and mechanisms protruding from between the claws. He had not even had his hearing aid for twenty-four hours and he had destroyed it, and we had not yet sent in the insurance papers.

I took a swallow of coffee and calmly asked, "What happened?"

"He told me to make sure I cleaned the aid every morning before I put it back in my ear, so I picked it up in the hook to do the job, and it clamped down completely."

On Monday morning he visited the audiologist's office again.

"I've had people who have told me that the dog ate their hearing aid or they dropped it down the toilet, but this is the first time I've had someone crush their brand new device beyond repair while trying to clean it," Dr. Sheffey said, seemingly trying hard to decide whether or not to let a smile make its way to his lips.

༄

In all the years of our marriage, I have needed to give direct nursing care to John on only two occasions, both occurring after he underwent left eye blepharoplasty, a kind of plastic surgery involving the repositioning of the eyebrow. Since his injury severed part of the nerve on the left side of his face, he has never been able to raise his left eyebrow or give a wide-eyed gaze as he can do on the right side of his face. The left side of his mouth also droops and even when he tries he cannot fully smile on that side. At about twenty year intervals his left eyebrow has drooped so much as to interfere with his peripheral vision and the lid and eye have become very irritated when his seasonal allergies flair up.

The remedy for this condition is to get a brow lift, but in his case only the left eye gets done. Because the eyebrow will eventually droop again after surgery, on both occasions the plastic surgeon has lifted those facial elements higher than the corresponding ones on the right side of his face, giving him the appearance of exaggerated asymmetry for a year or so, then his normal symmetry resumes as the left brow eases onto the same plane as the right one, then it droops again as the surgical benefits reach their expected end-point. After both of these surgeries John needed me to regularly change the ice packs needed to keep down the swelling, and occasionally to apply a new bandage to the operative site, neither of which jobs necessarily require an advanced degree in nursing.

I, however, have had quite a few fixer-uppers, including having total knee joint replacements in both legs, done seven years apart. With the permanent insertion of these artificial joints it means that at any one time I actually am equipped with more prosthetic devices than he is, but mine are implanted within my body while his are removable. For the five years before I had my first knee replacement I wore a full-leg hinged knee brace, and for three months prior to that surgery I was in so much bone-on-bone pain, I had to use a walker for assistance and sometimes needed the use of an electric motor cart to shop for groceries or a wheelchair to go to a mall.

John was a willing driver of the latter device, but he does not have a wheelchair adapted hook or hand, so he often would roll me forward and in a left-arcing circle, as his right hand dominated on the back of the chair. I would attempt to correct this imbalance by steering the wheel of the chair with my good left hand and arm. Ironically during this same period of time, I experienced a tear to my right shoulder rotator cuff, necessitating my wearing an arm immobilizer. On one occasion while I was wearing both the knee brace and the arm immobilizer and John was pushing me along the aisle of a mall, I watched as two women who saw us coming towards them moved out of the way. Apparently thinking we were deaf—maybe they saw our hearing aids—as well as disabled, one whispered rather loudly to the other, "I wonder what the car that hit those two looks like?"

჻

Even though my knee implants are titanium, which are not technically metal, there is apparently still enough metal in my body to set off all kinds of scanners. Prior to the availability in airports of comprehensive x-ray scanners I often had to get full body pat downs before boarding an aircraft. Nowadays when we travel together through airports, John may be in one line, taking off his arm and sending it through separately so he can then pass through the metal detector without setting off security alarms, while I am in another line also being scanned thoroughly by an x-ray machine for the TSA's fear of my hoarding too much metal.

During one of my most recent surgeries, a laminectomy—spinal surgery—I was discharged home with a twelve-inch waterproof bandage covering the surgical wound. We were told that the bandage would probably not need to be changed before the fifth day, at which point it could be removed for good, but as these things sometimes turn out, I had a lot of bleeding and needed to have a bandage change on the second day I was home. At discharge a nurse had shown me a videotape of the correct way to change the bandage, which was made from double-side sticky tape encircling absorbent material. She said anyone nearby could assist me in doing this, and to be on the safe side she sent me home with four brand new sets of the bandage.

John was very solicitous of my recovery and when it became apparent that I would need to have the dressing changed, he assured me he could do this—after all, he reminded me, he had two graduate degrees. Since I could do nothing for myself regarding this bandage maneuver to my lower back, my role was to instruct him, recounting the videotape that I had watched all the way through twice in the hospital while I was still under the influence of heavy drugs. We set up everything on the bedside table and he prepared to go to work as nursing assistant.

As he left our house to return to the surgical center for more bandages, it occurred to me that it is never a really good idea to let a one-armed nurse change a dressing like this, no matter how good his intentions are.

Our daughter, Elizabeth, is very musical, having played the piano, flute, and piccolo in early school years, then the marimba and other percussion instruments in college bands. As a busy young mother, she continues to play the flute and piccolo in her church choir and in community band concerts, and her children seem to have inherited some of her musical ability, with one playing the guitar and one the violin. While our son is not especially musical, his son, our oldest grandson, plays several varieties of guitar and is in a garage band.

The sole contributor to musicality in our children is John. Since his childhood he has sung, first as a boy soprano and then as a baritone in high school and college glee clubs and musicals, and later as a member of the bass section in several church choirs. But the music he most enjoyed was playing his guitar. He remembers listening for hours to early Flatt and Scruggs instrumentals and copying the special styles of both legendary artists. I have never heard him play guitar but can imagine he would be totally absorbed in practicing until he could produce the same kind of sounds as his role models. Once at a craft show we considered buying him a hammered dulcimer, which requires little two-handed effort, but he declined, saying he would rather have his memories than to try to play a new instrument.

We have kept the piano from our daughter's childhood. Every Christmas John pulls out from the piano bench her old sheet music of Christmas carols, accompanying himself on vocals as he plays the melody with his right hand and hits single piano keys of the chords with the prongs of his hook. I adore hearing him do "Hark the Herald Angels Sing" and "Away in a Manger." At this stage of our life, he is also asked frequently to lead the singing of "How Great Thou Art" or "Amazing Grace" at funerals for our friends and families.

I much prefer the Christmas caroling.

In psychiatric language, the things people fear are called phobias and the things people love are called philias. There is acrophobia (fear of heights) and arachnophobia (fear of spiders) and anglophilia (love of all things English) and bibliophilia (love of books). If a person spends time investing in or repeating the unusual behavior beyond what a normal person might do then the person is said to have a fetish and/or to be a devotee.

People who have an intense fear of amputations are said to have apotemnophobia, and those who want to become amputees themselves or who want to look like amputees are apotemnophiliacs (wannabes). To make matters more confusing, those *people who have an intense sexual interest in amputees* but *no desire to become one themselves* are classified as acrotomophiliacs. Wikipedia allocates eight pages to descriptions of and treatment for apotemnophilia and three pages to the phenomenon of acrotomophilia.

Some adults have used the theme of apotemnophobia to discourage certain sexual practices, like self-stimulation, telling generations of pubescent boys that such behavior will cause the hand to fall off. So-called shock rocker Marilyn Manson used the theme of amputations in his song, "Dream of Amputation," and his stage props, playing off the fear of amputations, often include surgical implements which add to his image as an anti-establishment gore performer.

While web sites offering mainstream information for amputees do exist, there are also numerous web sites for amputee devotees, wannabes, and for those who fear amputations. Ian Gregson, an above-knee amputee and Paralympian who is now a political activist and writer living in Canada, says he first learned about wannabes when he searched the young Internet in 1994 looking for amputee oriented resources available online. To his surprise the only material he could locate was an FTP (file transfer protocol) site in Texas which "was a devotee/amputee server dedicated to supplying pictures of amputees to those with a sexual attraction to amputees." From that initiation, Gregson discovered the existence of fetish devotees and he says a lot of encounters he had experienced in amputee sports events began to make sense for him. In 1997, *Hustler* magazine published "Humping Stumps," Gregson's controversial and occasionally erotic non-fiction account of men and women devotees and the extreme measures that some have taken to become amputees. For instance, "a man in Florida who had had enough of his life as a biped picked up a 12-guage rifle, put the barrel to his left knee and pulled the trigger. The man is now a self-proclaimed happy-go-lucky above-knee amputee," Gregson wrote.

Some acrotomophiliacs hide their interest, even though their choice of a marital partner is an amputee. Others can become fixated or obsessed and may become pests or may stalk amputees. Most acrotomophiliacs are very open and in this case the attraction reportedly works out well for both persons as long as the interest goes beyond an affinity for the stump. Ilse Martin, a woman born with missing or malformed limbs, wrote her thesis about this phenomenon, "differentiating between those acrotomophiliacs with a tendency to reduce a person to their disability and those who regard their disabled partners as a whole person. She "feels that it is important to free serious acrotomophiliacs from their dirty image... that the 'bad guys' are the most visible and fearful... but only a small category of acrotomophiliacs fall into this category."

John has played amputee golf for more than thirty-five years, and he is not aware of ever having had an encounter with a wannabe or a devotee in those settings. On more than one social occasion, however, male friends of John's have noticed the exaggerated phallic resemblance of his stump and have suggested that he would probably have no need for Viagra™ with a piece of built in equipment like that. One female friend (maybe there are more who have never confessed) has expressed her erotic interest in the stump. She always couches her interest in a joke, but one wonders how serious she is and hopes she will not openly become a devotee nor maim herself or someone else in pursuit of a stump. At any rate, John's stump is not for hire, or even for rent.

Other than in the devotee forums and in a few scientific articles about the fetish aspect of amputee sex, depictions of sex and amputees are rarely addressed in medical or popular literature. An exception is the small sex scene played by the characters Wendy and Dean in "Stick a Fork in Me," (C A Powers, 2009). They exemplify the dilemma some amputee/normie couples face in their relationship relative to the role of the artificial limb in a couples sex life. In the story, Phase

One of Wendy and Dean's relationship, which was very loving, lasted until Wendy got her prosthetic arm, which author Powers describes as "pretty realistic looking, (having) a synthetic material that imitated skin, and it fit her shoulder comfortably. Dean was interested in the arm at first. He just wouldn't watch her take it off at night. If Wendy wanted to have sex, Dean made her leave it on. Then once in the throes of passion, she hit him with the arm and broke his nose. He lost interest in sex."

Years ago in our attempt to become askable parents to our young children, John and I enrolled in a parenting and sexuality class at our church. Anticipating a need for ice-breaking around a number of sexual topics, the instructor asked each participant to speak about a sexual word chosen at random from a pile of index cards. We sat in a circle with several other parents, and as the words penis, vagina, orgasm, and others were spoken, all went well. Then a man across the circle from John selected the word masturbation. He began to explain how he had been told as a child that engaging in such behavior might cause him to lose his hand. John stealthily removed the prosthetic hand and pointed to his stump, solemnly nodded, then said, "It's true."

I have been sexually interested in John for more than 47 years, but I lost interest in the stump as an object of arousal after about the first kiss. Sometimes people want to know if John has a special arm or hand for sex. No, he just gets naked like everybody else, but he has hit me in the eye with his prosthesis while we were dining out. On that occasion he had turned to see something behind him and was not aware of where his prosthesis was leading him. I did not lose interest in sex or dining out because of this, but I did have a black eye for a few days.

శౌ

In the fall of 2005, John and I had just spent an exhausting two weeks in England, where we had gone to see his stepmother, Jean, who had recently moved into a nursing home there, and to have a little holiday after the stopover with her. While we were visiting Jean, she died unexpectedly and I was the only person who witnessed her death. Tragic as that was for all of us, it was made even more complicated for John and me because the unanticipated death prompted a coroner's inquest into the circumstances of her death.

On the third day after her death, while listening to me being questioned by the coroner for the second time, John experienced the sudden onset of an irregular heartbeat. Reflecting upon this event, he said it occurred to him, while hearing the questioning, that I might be kept in a British prison for the rest of my life. He said it felt to him as though he had been hit in the chest by a lightning bolt. He looked at me with tears pooling and said, "I couldn't stand it if something were to happen to you."

While he was initially shaken, he quickly recovered his composure which did not falter through the rest of the trip. By the time we left the U.K. for home, the inquest had not been concluded, thus there was still some talk of me being a "person of interest." John's heartbeat remained erratic, and upon returning home, we sought medical advice at the University hospital near our home.

As usually happens when a heart patient arrives in an emergency department, all forces mustered to get John into an examining room and to be seen quickly by the resident physician. This doctor quickly ascertained from the heart monitor that John's heartbeat was indeed irregular, and he began to examine him for other symptoms. He asked him to grin and grimace and noted the asymmetry of his face. To assess John's grip the doctor asked John to squeeze both of the doctor's hands with each of his own hands. John failed that part of the exam, too. The physician told us he thought he had better order a CAT scan of the brain, since there were several initial signs of a possible stroke.

Thirty minutes later, the excited doctor informed us that he had seen the CAT scan and there was no stroke, but that part of John's brain was missing. We told him we already knew that. He referred us to a cardiologist in an outpatient visit several weeks down the road.

As we sat in the cardiologist's office waiting for the results of the many pre-appointment tests John had gone through, we watched the nurse practitioner going over all the records in preparation for the specialist's arrival in the room. Suddenly she said, "Oh my gosh, this is terrible. This is the worst thing I have ever seen. Oh, this is awful."

Fearing she was finding serious issues with the yet-unknown-to-us test results, I stopped her and asked what the matter was.

"I'm reading here the account from the ER physician, and it says, 'This man has just returned to the U.S. from England, and his heart problem started the moment he and his wife were arrested for the murder of his stepmother.'"

The irregular heartbeat eventually cleared up on its own. Three months after Jean's death the coroner's inquest was completed, showing she had died suddenly and unpredictably of natural causes. The cardiologist decided John had experienced a kind of temporary condition that comes from extreme emotional stress and that can cause occasional but non-serious irregular heart rhythms. It does beg the question, though, about who in this cast of characters, might have had part of their brain missing.

᭑

It was an especially hot early September day in Washington when John and I visited the National Mall, where we had never before been. First pausing to absorb the impact of the Vietnam Memorial Wall, with the names of the more than 58,000 men and women who died in that tragic conflict, we then walked on slowly past it to another bronze monument set under a canopy of trees. This one featured three figures, two female armed forces nurses wearing fatigues and an injured serviceman whom they were attending.

I was waiting for my second total knee joint replacement, scheduled for the following week, and I crept along slowly, pushing in front of me a walker. John, whose walking pace is always measured in jet-speed, uncharacteristically hung back to stay at my side as we made our way to the Vietnam Women's Memorial, the only national monument dedicated to remembering the women, especially the nurses, who served in the Vietnam War. It had taken Diane Carlson Evans, a registered nurse member of the Army Nurse Corps from 1966-1972 and who served in Vietnam in 1968-69, ten years from idea to actuality to see this memorial dedicated in 1993.

John was wearing his hook prosthesis and I imagine we truly looked to a casual observer as though we were candidates for Disabled Couple of the Year. We were the only people at the monument just then, and we walked around it slowly, taking in the power of that frozen-in-time scene which surely had been replayed thousands of times in that war and many others.

Beginning quietly and then becoming more vocal as he found his rhythm, John began to tell me for the first time in detail, what it had meant to him to be cared for at Moody and later at Lackland's Wilford Hall Hospital by the registered nurses there.

"The nurses are the ones who really got me through," he said. "They were the very best. They knew when to push and when to lay back and they took no guff. They were thoroughly professional at every step."

I began to sniffle, then to openly cry. My knee was hurting so we moved over to a nearby bench and sat down. A man who we had not previously noticed walked over to us from where he had been standing at the edge of the paved area. We involuntarily recoiled, not knowing what he might be selling or worse, fearing that he might be intending to harm us. Instead he put out his hand to John and said, "Thanks for your service." Then he turned and disappeared.

I totally lost it, burying my head in John's soft shoulder while I sobbed and he patted me. After recovering my composure to some degree, I found myself looking to those bronzed nurses just in front of us who were cradling the service man, and I said to them, "Thanks for your service, too."

Up in the air

John loves flying in a way I can never truly understand. For me an airplane is a vehicle that carries people from one place to another by ascending over terrain and then coming back down. For him, flying planes, especially jet aircraft, is about the thrill that comes with being master of a powerful machine and guiding it gracefully through skies of blue, then landing carefully on an airstrip.

Periodically during the first twenty years of our marriage, John flew small rental planes by taking a flight qualification checkout at an airport near where we lived. Flying these planes could be done under VFR (visual flight rules) or IFR (instrument flight rules), depending on the weather conditions.

Milwaukee is only about ninety miles north of Chicago—an hour and one-half car ride in 1968 from our door to his father's home, but for John it was much more interesting to commute by air. On August 30, 1968, piloting a Piper Arrow Constant Speed Turbo-charged retractable gear four passenger aircraft, he flew out of Sylvania Airport in Sturdevant in far southeast Wisconsin, his flight log shows, with four-month old daughter Elizabeth in the rear seat and me in the copilot seat. Taxiing to the east runway, he lifted off over Lake Michigan under VFR and turned south. Paralleling Lake Shore Drive with the approach over the Navy Pier, we could easily see boats of all sizes cruising and moored along the lakefront. We landed twenty-five minutes later at Meigs Field located at the edge of Lake Michigan near his father's residence.

His flying wings were clipped while we lived in Nevada after we left Illinois—it costs a fair amount of money to fund the habit—but after we got re-established in Tennessee he was up in the air again. Before the year 2000, major league football frequently held exhibition games in cities around the globe as ways to increase their visibility and to promote goodwill. Our son, Jon, was a huge Pittsburgh Steelers fan, especially favoring Terry Bradshaw. The Steelers, with Bradshaw at the helm, scheduled a game against the New England Patriots in Neyland Stadium in August 1982, coinciding with the World's Fair in Knoxville.

In early summer we bought tickets for the four of us to attend the August 14 game and anticipation in our household was high. By the second week of August, however, we knew Jon, aged twelve, could not attend the game. He was diagnosed with osteomyelitis in his left ankle, an infection in the marrow of the bone, and he spent three weeks in the hospital receiving intravenous antibiotics. Once discharged, he wore an orthopedic boot on the foot and had to continue on medication for six months. Despite his great disappointment, doctors said he could not travel. John invited another father and his daughter to go to the game with him and Elizabeth in Jon's and my place.

The two fathers and daughters left in a Piper Arrow with John piloting on the 14th just after lunch. They flew the 179 miles from Smyrna Airport to Knoxville's Island Home Airport (officially known as Knoxville Downtown Island Airport) in calm weather on VFR, landing in just under an hour. Located less than one-half mile from Neyland Stadium, the Island Home airport was a busy facility that afternoon and night. The Steelers won 24-20. Returning to Smyrna Airport from Knoxville was a little trickier in the fog that by now had engulfed the Middle Tennessee area, so John switched from VFR to IFR for vectoring into Smyrna. A few weeks later, he took Jon and our nephew, Steve, up in the Piper Arrow for a sightseeing jaunt around Middle Tennessee.

There is one aircraft, however, in which John refuses to ascend, even though I and several of our friends chose to do so.

"I will never get in any kind of flying contraption that does not have wings," he said as the others of us prepared to ascend in a hot air balloon over Park City, Utah on the Fourth of July in 2000.

Watching him grow smaller as we lifted further off the ground, I marveled that I was the one taking the chance while he—the consummate risk-taker in our relationship—chose to man the chase vehicle. An hour later, when we had descended in a school yard that was not exactly our target, I began to understand why wings might be important.

In January 2012, John was chosen as one of a dozen men from Nashville and other cities to spend two days and one night aboard the USS George H. W. Bush (CVN 77), one of ten Nimitz-class nuclear-powered carriers in the U.S. fleet. The Bush, named for the first President Bush, who served in World War II at age eighteen as the still-youngest-ever naval aviator, was cruising ninety miles off the coast of Virginia, en route back to Naval Station Norfolk, which supports the operational readiness of the US Atlantic Fleet, providing facilities and services to enable mission accomplishment. The Bush was returning stateside from its first deployment in the Mideast.

Ahead of its scheduled arrival in home port a few weeks hence, the Bush was tracing a circuitous course in the Atlantic Ocean, while young naval aviators from various bases, who would soon be assigned to our nation's combat fleet, were qualifying for carrier aviation status by practicing landings and take offs from its deck. While the carrier was in this non-combat mode, several groups of civilians were invited to spend time aboard the ship as part of the Navy's public affairs program—the Distinguished Visitor Embark—created to acquaint citizens with certain naval operations, in hopes they in turn would tell folks back home about the navy.

Only the best of the naval aviators who begin flight school emerge as carrier-eligible pilots. Each carrier aviator-candidate must qualify with ten daylight and six nighttime arrested (commonly called tail hook) landings and catapult assisted take-offs, in all kinds of weather. During a carrier landing, a hook drops down from under the tail of the plane and grabs one of three possible cables splayed across the deck of the vessel, stopping the plane abruptly.

Any of the three cables will do the job, but the targeted objective among flyers is to catch the second, or middle, cable. Because of the possibility that the hook might not catch *any* cable or that it may fail to stay engaged, the planes, which decelerate at speeds from 105 to 0 mph in two seconds, are not powered down until they are completely stopped on the deck. Should a hook fail, the plane continues forward on the deck and is immediately back in the air, from where the aviator makes a long turn and gets in line to try another tail hook landing. Because of the inherent risk of a crash at sea, naval rescue helicopters hover over the water during each round of launches or landings.

After spending some down time onboard, each aviator must successfully take off from the short catapult-empowered runway, a maneuver requiring great coordination and skill on the part of both the aviators and the ground crews. Everything that happens in these take-offs and landings is choreographed to the minutest detail. The crucial final players in this sequence are the aviator seated under the closed canopy of the cockpit and the launch seaman, called the shooter, who is positioned on deck about thirty feet to the right or left side of the plane, within clear view of the pilot.

The aviator receives the engine run-up hand signal from the shooter and then gives him a confirmatory salute. The shooter then drops to his knees on the deck and signals for takeoff, a motion resembling the stance of a birddog on point. This signal tells another seaman to release the launch cable, which causes the nose of the plane to dip slightly. With this dipping motion, everyone knows this is a launch. When the plane is released, the heads of all on board the plane are momentarily jerked back, as if they had just been hurled from a slingshot. This entire launch sequence takes three seconds and by then the plane has accelerated from zero to one-hundred twenty-eight miles per hour.

While John had often experienced touch and go landings as a jet pilot, Air Force pilots do not make carrier landings. At age seventy, he was more than excited about having the opportunity to add this to "checked-off" on his bucket list, even if he could not be in the pilot's seat. He barely slept the night before departure. He flew commercially to Norfolk, where he spent a night in the Navy Lodge. Bright and early next morning he and his fellow participants were briefed on the tarmac, and then they suited up in life vests and helmets.

They were strapped securely into a C-2 Greyhound, called a POD, a twenty-five passenger navy transport airplane and flown for thirty minutes towards the huge carrier, grabbing tail hook cable two in a perfect at-sea landing. For the rest of that day and night and half of the next day, John and the other civilians were briefed about our country's naval mission by the ship's captain, the fleet admiral, and other men and women representing the 6000 sailors and aviators who live and work aboard the Bush.

The day they arrived the weather was gorgeous and the ocean was smooth as glass. Watching from on-deck positions and from the bridge, the visitors learned many of the fine points of carrier operations, including especially the takeoff and landing procedures. Even as John tried to sleep on the bottom bunk in his quarters directly under the carrier landing site, he felt and heard the rumble and roar of planes landing and taking off until midnight.

When they woke up the next morning, the civilian visitors saw the weather had substantially changed, with winds of fifty knots across the deck and ten foot swells in the sea. In such circumstances rescue helicopters cannot lift off, effectively grounding other planes from landing or taking off until the winds calm somewhat. After a delay of about an hour while the winds calmed, the POD flew in and landed, discharging about 25 passengers, including another ten or so invited citizens for that day's ship-board encounter.

As the rain pelted them and their luggage, which was sitting on the ship's launch deck beside the POD, the civilians in John's group, along with several now-qualified pilots and other crew members boarded the plane and were tightly secured in their seats. Their soggy luggage was stowed and they were briefed on the basics of a catapult assisted take-off. As they were launched, John felt the nose of the POD dip and his head was momentarily pinned to his headrest as the plane was thrust off the carrier. Thirty minutes later they touched down at Naval Station Norfolk, and in another twenty-four hours everyone had returned to their home cities.

It took John several weeks to debrief from this once in a lifetime adventure, where according to the Honorary Tailhooker certificate he received, he "gained an elementary understanding of the remarkable challenges and accomplishments of Naval Aviation, a patriotic profession that has helped keep the nation free since the early 1900's."

In the captain's seat on USS George H. W. Bush

The experience was made even more special a week or so later when he received photos and video shot by several of the other participants. Seemingly still up in a cloud as he relived each piece of the trip, he told me, "This had to be one of the top experiences in my life."

"Better than marrying me?" I teased.

His sheepish grin told me that was an answer I did not want to know.

After not flying for more than fifteen years, John stopped getting annual flight physicals in 2002, effectively retiring his pilot's license. Even so, every time we step onto a commercial carrier, I can see him going through the cockpit mental checklist that was such a part of his life when he sat in the pilot's seat himself. Although he doesn't usually do so, if he happens to converse with the flight crew as we are boarding, he mentally sizes up the chances that the pilot and co-pilot might have been military pilots. Any other training, he believes, renders a commercial pilot less effective. His beliefs were confirmed in 2008 when Captain Sullenberger, a former Air Force pilot, nestled the US Airways plane he was piloting when it collided mid-air with geese safely in the Hudson River with no casualties on board.

He subscribes to the quarterly newsletter of the National Transportation Safety Board (NTSB) whose job is to investigate all aircraft accidents in the United States and to report the findings about cause and casualties. John's habit is to stack all these publications in a pile for reading when he is traveling, like on an airplane, and it can be a little daunting to be seated next to him on a commercial flight when he pulls out the NTSB Report and digests the post-mortem on any recent air tragedy. To John, though, it is as routine and unemotional as to me watching a wound being stitched together in the emergency room or hearing the gruesome details of a friend's recent surgery. It's what we were trained to do and what we will probably do without a flicker for the rest of our lives, or so I thought about myself until recently.

November 22, 2013 marked fifty years since the assassination of President John F. Kennedy in Dallas. I was a sophomore nursing major at the time of his death. Just six months before that awful day I had been in the football stadium at Vanderbilt University where the President, visiting Middle Tennessee to help open the dam at the newly created Percy Priest Lake east of Nashville, addressed a crowd of thousands. He had been invited to Vanderbilt by our then-newly installed chancellor, Dr. Alexander Heard, a contemporary and friend of Kennedy.

Eighteen-year-olds often have big dreams and for this eighteen-year old girl, just barely a year out of high school, seeing Kennedy in person was a Camelot dream comes true. A few months later, I was in Washington on the day Dr. King gave his "I have a dream" speech, but I did not hear or see him. My brother was a Secret Service agent in the White House then and he advised me to go to the other end of D.C.

that day because there was likely to be trouble from all the folks getting stirred up by these speeches. My brother was right—hearing such inspirational talks translated into a belief for my generation that living our dreams was within our grasps.

When the news of Kennedy's being shot and later his death at Parkland Hospital reached the Vanderbilt campus that cold November Friday, I felt I might never again dream the kind of dreams I had up until then. Deep inside I also vowed to go to work at Parkland when I graduated in 1966. Somehow it seemed I might be able to redeem a little of the Kennedy dream if I worked in the setting where he had died.

A couple of my classmates felt the same pull to Parkland as I had and during Spring Break of our senior year we made a pilgrimage to Dallas, having secured job interviews with Mrs. Goode, the director of nursing. While in Dallas the night before my interview I became violently ill, and my friend drove me to the ER at Parkland. The nurses efficiently triaged me to surgery services and the resident who saw me ordered that I be admitted with suspected appendicitis and scheduled me for emergency surgery. I transitioned to the surgery floor and was given pre-op meds, but when I awoke, I had not undergone surgery—an attending physician had further reviewed my case and determined I most likely had food poisoning. I was to be observed for a couple more days and if I improved I could be discharged. Mrs. Goode conducted my job interview at bedside and I flew home on Saturday with my appendix intact.

Two of us from my nursing class eventually began work at Parkland in August after our graduation. I stayed at Parkland less than a year, working the graveyard shift in the MICU and taking other shifts in the SICU and occasionally the Emergency Department. My time there was full of drama and sadness and more experience than I could have imagined in a lifetime, including a brief stint of having Jack Ruby admitted to Parkland from the Dallas County Jail as a terminal cancer patient, where he died in early January 1967. I learned to "suck it up," as folks say today, keeping my feelings deep inside and doing what needed to be done, whether that was to hold pressure over a gunshot wound erupting blood from the femoral artery while the wife and girlfriend of the patient continued their warfare outside the door to the room or to participate in one of the frequent Code Blues. That's what a nurse does.

I had passed through Dallas a few times in the forty-seven years since I left Parkland, but I had never visited the Book Depository Building or Dealey Plaza or been back to Parkland any of those times. In January 2014 while visiting Lynne, a friend who lives in the area, we went one morning to the George W. Bush Presidential Library on the campus of Southern Methodist University. Afterwards we traveled to the West End of downtown Dallas and ate lunch, before crossing several more streets and entering the Sixth Floor Museum. Inside this now emptied Texas school book storehouse, we rode the freight elevator to the sixth floor and saw the somber reality of Oswald's clear view of the motorcade. On display were exact replicas of the weapon used by the killer and of the camera used by Mr. Zapruder to film the only complete account of the crime. The taped video of Walter Cronkite reporting Kennedy's death and the newspaper accounts brought the moments back in vivid reality.

A couple days later my flight home departed from Dallas Love Field and I asked Lynne to drive out Harry Hines Boulevard by Parkland before dropping me at the nearby airport. So many outlying structures are now in place that the Parkland image I remembered could not be seen. At any rate, a brand new Parkland is rising across Harry Hines and it was good to see the old being renewed.

By chance, once I was through security in Love Field, I met my son, Jon, who was also connecting for a business trip through Love Field. I rarely get an opportunity to visit with him without hundreds of other distractions, so having an hour in the restaurant while he grabbed lunch was the perfect ending to a great Texas visit. He asked if I had seen the recent movie *Parkland* which had debuted a few months earlier. "You can download it on I-Tunes," he said.

On a cold January night a few weeks after having stood in the window space of the Sixth Floor Museum, I watched *Parkland* on my home computer. Scenes of the actual assassination filmed by Mr. Zapruder were interspersed with 1963 newsreels, and re-enactments of events in the Emergency Room used actual or staged interior and exterior shots of Parkland.

During my time at Parkland, I only knew a couple of the staff portrayed in the film. Everyone who worked there at the time knew of Mrs. Nelson, the larger-than-life nursing supervisor of the ER but I really only knew her to see her. With the passage of years I would not have been able to verify any identities from the film portrayals. However, the images of the trauma team and their efforts to save the President seemed spot on to my memory of the way things were done three years later when I was there. I was completely absorbed in reminiscing about the primitive state of the art of trauma care in 1963 and especially the abandonment of any efforts at sterile precautions as everyone there tried to do what was not possible in this particular case.

The film recreated the ER scenes from testimony given by people who were there to the Warren Commission and other investigations. In one scene, the actress playing Jackie Kennedy is standing next to the gurney on which her husband is lying. Various doctors have just described their findings after examining the President's wounds. "Part of his skull and brain is missing," someone barks, at which point Jackie turns to Mrs. Nelson and opens her cupped hands, showing the skull fragments and brain matter she had retrieved in the car after the bullets' impact and had desperately protected during the trip to Parkland. Mrs. Nelson receives the tissue and bone in a basin and turns away from the trauma team, knowing as everyone in the room knows that these missing parts can never be put back in place.

All this action occurred in just a few seconds, but I was undone by the scene, sobbing in great wails as I saw in my mind's eye for the first time my own husband's skull fragments and brain matter exploding from his head at impact with the propeller.

Peter Rosenberger writes in the February 2012 *Middle Tennessee Health and Wellness Magazine*,"(r)aising a family and keeping love alive in a marriage with a spouse who is constantly sick or in severe pain is an extreme challenge; one with many casualties. The divorce rate in couples with a disability in the family hovers around ninety percent, and relationships with a disability or chronic medical condition daily face significant pressures on the love holding the marriage together."

We have not had the challenge of a spouse constantly sick or in severe pain, but we do know about living with a disability and we have tasted the stress of chronic pain. During two recent years I was in severe pain such that I almost took my life—and briefly, almost took John's, also. For a year and a half I had had a chronic pain syndrome that could not be diagnosed. I had seen six medical specialists and had been treated with narcotic and non-narcotic medications, had received so much physical therapy that I had maxed out on benefits, had had the area injected with steroid and numbing injections, and I began to feel as if I were going crazy.

The pain had been localized initially on the side of my left buttock in an area no larger than a half-dollar but later the tender area also ran along the outside of my left upper leg. Eventually it reached the point where even lightly touching it caused exquisite tenderness. There was nothing to see or feel, like a growth or a mass, in the tender area and neither CAT scans nor MRI's nor x-rays revealed any cause for my misery. By late spring 2013 the pain was so bad I could barely walk more than a few hundred feet and I could feel my muscles beginning to atrophy—to shrink from lack of use.

I could be distracted from the pain most of the time during the day, but shortly after getting to sleep every night it woke me up and then for most of every night I was up wandering through our darkened house or sitting in a chair in the den thinking of ways to end my life. It is easy for me to understand how sleep deprivation is used as a kind of mental torture. After weeks or maybe only days of not sleeping, a person changes. Nerves are frayed and perspectives shift and for me, my personality moved to a person I hardly knew.

On two occasions, triggered by the smallest annoyance from something John said or did, I lit into him, once verbally and once physically. He is much stronger and larger than me so there was never any chance I could overpower him, but the ferocity of my attack and the complete loss of control terrified me. When we were to the other side of this crisis and could look back and reflect, John said, "You are lucky I have a good sense of humor because anyone else would have called the police and had you arrested."

೪

Richard Needham writes, "You don't marry one person; you marry three: the person you think they are, the person they are, and the person they are going to become as a result of being married to you." Our lives together were merged so quickly that I don't believe either of us had much opportunity to consider these three options, but I also believe each of us intuitively knew these three aspects about the other. In fact, on our wedding day I gave John the Carl Sandburg poem about love which I had committed to memory years earlier and which captures the essence of Needham's statement.

> "I love you. I love you for what you are, but I love you yet more for what you are going to be. I love you not so much for your realities as for your ideals. I pray for your desires, that they may be great, rather than for your satisfactions, which may be so hazardously little.

> "A satisfied flower is one whose petals are about to fall. But the most beautiful rose is one, hardly more than a bud, wherein the

pangs and ecstasies of desire are working for
larger and finer growth. Not always shall you
be what you are now. You are going forward
toward something great. I am on the way
with you and... I love you."

My life with John has been nothing like the one I
imagined for myself when I was twenty-two. Then I
viewed myself in the future being married to someone
who was rather conventional and traditional and with
whom I would probably live a rather unremarkable
life, as generations of my ancestors had done before
me. John says his life has been nothing like he
expected, either. At twenty-five he did not ever see
himself being married or having children. For him life
was supposed to be about high-flying adventures and
nothing tying him down.

Recently I listened as he told some new friends
about why he married me—why he gave up the
expense account, the five-star hotels, the travels to
exotic places and access to unlimited foods and drink.
Why he changed from the most confirmed bachelor
ever into a husband in such short order. And why he
has stayed in that role for forty-eight years. He said he
had dated lots of women. Some of these companions
were short trysts and some were a little longer but
when he met me there was something there—a spirit
or spark that he had never before encountered.

He saw in me a streak of independence, of
confidence,   of   competitiveness—qualities   that
instinctively he knew were a good match for him. He
saw in me a person of honor, of competency—a person

who would hold his feet to the fire. He also experienced me as "not clingy." I was someone who kept her feelings to herself and did not ask much of him in that realm. He said most all the other women he'd known were pouty and tried to draw him into their sphere with tears. I was one who could have fun but could also be serious. He told the group that he loved me from the day he met me. After I left him in St. Moritz and traveled to Rome before returning to the U.S., his life did not look the same anymore, he said, and he knew he had to return to the states and marry me.

I saw in him a person who cared about family. The racial riots that racked the U.S. in 1967 were erupting in New Jersey about the time we met. His mother and brother were living on the Jersey shore very near to Asbury Park, which was burned and looted almost to the point of no return. While we were together in Europe, he remarked to me that he worried about them, especially at the distance where he was from them.

A few months later I saw him and his brother laughing together in a way I had never known in my family. He knew how to play and even though I had just spent three months playing, I knew life going forward after this temporary oasis would be serious. If I married him, one of his jobs in our life would be to see that I played enough—and laughed enough.

He told me then he did not want to be emotionally very close, and that was fine with me at the time. I had my guard up and I was thankful that this was not a person who wanted to know my vulnerabilities or deepest feelings—or even my more surface ones. *Let's leave intimacy to someone else,* thought I.

All of that was enough for us to look one another in the eye in September 1967 and pledge to be each other's keeper until death did us part. We have both kept our part of the deal and more, learning along the way about our own and the other's insecurities and longings and successes and failures—our vulnerabilities and fears and our strengths and courage. About twenty-five years into our marriage, we began having face-to-face chat time for an hour a day, usually at about 4:30 in the afternoon. We call it tea time and it gives us an opportunity to talk about how each other's day has gone and to get under the surface of anything that we may need to explore. Intimacy is in fact a very good thing to have in our relationship, we discovered.

Because I am an AfterWife I did not know him when he was the consummate high school jock nor when he was an Air Force pilot, but I believe his athletic prowess is as much a part of his makeup as later on was his thirst for being a pilot. Both pursuits require enormous talent honed by thousands of hours of repetitive practice, and most importantly a fire in the belly to compete—to be the best—the top gun or the star athlete.

Sometimes I catch my breath and marvel at all we have experienced. At other times I think we have had almost nothing happen, especially in comparison to some of our friends and family whose jobs and health and marriages have gone far awry of their hopes and dreams. While we have experienced some pretty low moments and also some roller-coaster rides, from this viewpoint I think I have received far more than I could have dreamed of receiving. I am not grateful for his accident or the amputation or any of the other struggles that either of us has contributed to the relationship, but I *am* grateful for the relationship. The actress Joanne Woodward has said, "Sexiness wears thin after a while and beauty fades, but to be married to a man who makes you laugh every day, ah, now that's a real treat."

John has made me laugh almost every day.

Afterword

In 2013 the media was temporarily abuzz with a story about the return of an amputated arm to a Vietnamese man after almost fifty years of separation.

"US doctor returns amputated arm to Vietnamese veteran" ran the headline in the Telegraph. "An American doctor has arrived in Vietnam carrying an unlikely piece of luggage: the bones of an arm he amputated in 1966."

Dr. Sam Axelrad was a military surgeon in 1966 when Nguyen Quang Hung was brought to him with his right arm almost at the point of falling off from having been shot by a US sniper 3 days earlier. Dr. Axelrad amputated the limb above the elbow. Unknown to the doctor at the time, his assistants preserved the bones into a reconstructed skeletal forearm. When he left Vietnam he took the arm bones with him back to Texas where he practiced urology until his retirement some 40 years later. He did not look at the bones or any other Vietnam mementoes in his canvas duffle until 2011. When he discovered the arm bones he became curious to know to whom they had belonged and whether the owner were still alive. Hung was very much alive and almost 50 years after the arm was severed it was reunited with its owner in an emotional reunion with Axelrad's and Hung's family members in attendance in An Khe in the summer of 2013. Hung remarked he was glad he could eventually be buried with all his bones.

It is intriguing to think about the what ifs in a modern world. If John's accident occurred today, he would undoubtedly benefit from all of the modern technology and from the military's newer approaches to such situations. What if the surgeons could reattach the hand? If that did not work, what if he could be fitted with a sensor hand where the wrist and fingers operate independently and where almost no one can discern the difference between a normal limb and an artificial limb? What if he were a candidate for a hand transplant? What if instead of making a silicone ear for him to attach with glue or snaps, an actual matching ear could be grown in a Petri dish and then grafted on to his head? What if he could be returned to his flight squadron for rehab and then eventually be allowed to pilot for the Air Force?

He has always been curious about these new developments but never expected to benefit from them, since he is now in his seventies and he has been very satisfied with his level of function. Recently, however, the Nashville VA Audiology Clinic has evaluated him for a hearing aid that can be fitted to his left ear stump using micro-technology not previously available. Before the end of 2014 he will know if this evolving hearing science can help restore some of his ability to hear.

The Otto Bock Hand—Old Hand, I now call it— started to misbehave beginning in early 2014. One day it wouldn't open, the next it wouldn't close, then it wouldn't operate at all. It was sent for repairs four or five times and returned to the prosthetics office only to soon quit working again. One time it was returned in parts, having been repaired but not reassembled.

It misbehaved the whole time we were at the Amputee Tournament in New Jersey and later when we visited New York City. A few days after returning to our home from the Amputee tournament where I had seen the new naked bionic hand, I asked John again if he might be interested in getting one of these new devices. This time he said he might be, but he would need to know it could out perform his Old Hand, especially regarding strength. When his prosthetics vendor asked him the same question a few weeks later, adding that the VA had just been given authorization to begin using the new type hand and he could probably easily get approval for John, he agreed to give it a try. This particular brand, a different one than the man at the tourney represented, was made in Leeds, England, and then shipped to San Antonio where it was fitted into a socket similar to the one in Old Hand, he was told.

A few weeks later, authorization was received and John had measurements made for ordering his new B-Bionic hand. As is typical for government programs, however, there was a caveat. The government fiscal year ended September 30, and the order could not be placed until the new payment year began October 1. Once the hand was delivered to the prosthetic office, in December, all persons involved—in this case John, the prosthetic vendor, the company technician, several

VA physicians from the Amputee Clinic and various other official personnel—had to be present at one sitting to give the final authorization for John to receive the New Hand.

In the meantime he did not have Old Hand to rely upon and in frustration as he tried to do something with only one hand, he burst out," Dammit. I feel like a *!&^% handicapped person." Fed up, he finally called the Otto Bock customer service office and was met with great contrition that Old Hand had had to endure so much trouble. Almost by return mail, Old Hand came back to Nashville this time in tip top shape.

"That's the hand I've grown used to," said John. "It's very reliable."

I felt the same way.

On December 11, 2014, everyone necessary assembled at 10:00 AM in the Nashville VA clinic and the New Hand was unwrapped and tried on for the first time. I was unable to accompany him for this visit, which took over two hours he reported. The B-Bionic rep spent most of that time programming the microchip sensors and teaching John how to initiate and control the eight different movements New Hand is capable of making. Everyone agreed this would be a splendid new beginning for John and instructed him to make a return appointment after he had used New Hand for two months.

We were leaving on a five hour road trip immediately after his appointment so I had to delay my urge to see New Hand in action until we landed in our overnight accommodation. He then told me he needed time to practice by himself and he would show it to me in action the next day at lunch. I had family business to take care of the next morning and he stayed behind in the motel. When I picked him up for lunch without the fanfare he expected he immediately said, "You didn't notice I'm wearing my New Hand."

We chose a nearby deli restaurant and after we sat down in the booths to wait for our soup and salad to be delivered, he raised New Hand from under the table, placed it on the surface, and began to work the fingers. The first thing that struck me was that my husband had ten independent fingers now. With wonder in my voice, I kept repeating, "I've never known you with ten fingers—this will take some getting used to." The fingers and indeed the whole New Hand looked nothing like the artificial hand I'd been comfortable with for more than thirty years. This one looked like a real hand, but not like John's hand. He has a broad right hand with short thick fingers. New Hand was more elongated, with long thin fingers, each individually capable of movement and each with fingernails in need of being clipped. He had placed his college ring and watch on the New Hand, which gave it an air of some familiarity to me, but it did not look like my husband's hand.

He alternated wearing New Hand with wearing Old Hand all weekend while we were on the road, practicing using New Hand for holding both plastic and glass drink containers, a fork while he cut his meat, and an empty plate as if in a buffet line. After we got home he opened the piano and sat down to play some Christmas carols using New Hand's fingers but he quickly discovered he could only use the index finger set in the point mode and still did not have the mobility of a normie hand when trying to play chords so he stopped playing after *Away in a Manger*.

Feeling adequate in the social graces movements, he wore New Hand to a formal dinner complete with open bar and several buffet lines. Things went well with the red wine before dinner when New Hand behaved as expected, outdoing the old one with its ability to rotate so he could drink from the glass while holding it in New Hand. Then came time for the buffet line. New Hand was not up to the job when mashed potatoes and green beans were placed on the plate, which it released in to the chafing dish filled with beef stroganoff. John let out a curse. New Hand couldn't hold the fork as needed to slice into the chicken breast, and it couldn't hold his pants when he needed to button the placket. Then, worst case scenario, the next morning as he slipped his stump into New Hand's socket, there was a loud cracking sound and New Hand's casing snapped in two.

As I write this final chapter, New Hand is on its way back to San Antonio to have its socket remade— "stronger, much stronger," John instructed the prosthetics office. When John and New Hand are reunited John says he hopes the manufacturer's rep can do something to make the fingers grasp stronger also, like he has been used to for thirty plus years in Old Hand. Otherwise, I am afraid New Hand may never get much opportunity to meet all of the people who have said they want to make its acquaintance. It really doesn't matter much to me—I'm open to having a relationship with New Hand if need be, but I'm also quite comfortable with having Old Hand and its cousins, the Hooks in our armory.

In late 2014 John's left eyelid is starting to droop again—it's been almost ten years since his last lid lift so he went to see about getting it lifted again. "I wouldn't recommend it," his doctor told him. "For a person to have a third operation of this type the risks increase enormously. You could be blind or have extensive bleeding. If it were me, I wouldn't do it." Case settled.

The new VA hearing aids have arrived and are no more helpful for him than the single one he has been wearing, so he will keep that one in his good ear and use these for backups.

Some things never change. Some do.

The End

He loved her for almost everything she was

strong, competent, independent, defended, honest, self-reliant, dependable

And in his arms she became a little more

resilient, trusting, creative, other-reliant, receptive, vulnerable, loved

And she decided that was enough to let him stay for a very long time.

Mr. Right 1967-2015

Second, third, and fourth stanzas added by the author.

Note

"Will you love me still when I'm old and grey?" are lyrics from the song *Will you love me still*, written by Kathy Chiavola and Elizabeth Hill and recorded by Kathy on her *Harvest* CD (1996). Kathy has been a friend and we have been fans of hers since the early 1990's when her band played while we danced on stage for several years at the now defunct Summer Lights Festival in downtown Nashville. At that time John and I were members of a small buck dance troupe, the Music City Kicks, under the tutelage of Jacky Christian, a consummate old-time dancer and teacher. Kathy played at my 50th birthday party and whenever she plays in Nashville, usually at The Station Inn, we try to be there. She knows if she sees us I am itching to hear "Will you love me still when I'm old and grey?" among many other of our favorites she sings. The song has become a mantra for us of growing older together.

Acknowledgements

No book can be written without a circle of support. My circle for this book has many rings within.

At the innermost ring is my family--that into which I was born and into which I married and especially the family created with John. All of them have read the manuscript for this book and have added to the story with remembrances of their own. No one said I ought to remove any of the material in which they are mentioned. Thanks to daughter Elizabeth DeWerth, son Jon Manley, brother Scott Trundle, and brother-in-law Dick Manley for helping with the humor and also with the rescues. John has also read this entire book and while he is uncomfortable with some of the more personal profiles, he is not so uncomfortable to ask that I delete them. He is my beloved.

In the next ring are the people who have read or heard me read earlier versions of this story. The book was born in 2010 as a writing assignment in Victor Judge's class in the Osher Lifelong Learning Program at Vanderbilt. When he asked the attendees to do a free write on a topic of interest, the first thing that popped in to my mind was the humor of living with an amputee. I wrote a segment that was almost a synopsis of the finished book and when Victor read my essay to the class and they overwhelmingly laughed, I knew I was on to something. Working with other segments of the story, I shared pieces of it with various writing critique groups, gaining insight into what worked and also what troubled my listeners. One fellow writer expressed concern for what he thought was insensitivity on my part in that it might seem I was mocking amputees. That stopped me for a while as I considered the impact of what I was writing but then I determined that humor is what keeps most amps and their families going so I persevered.

Melody Lawrence, a literary critic in New York City whose acquaintance I made through Don Stickles, a mutual friend, read several draft versions and offered clear and precise critique that helped me to shape the story, and I am grateful for her professional and compassionate direction. A fellow writer and long-time friend and colleague, Alan Graber, read early drafts and even contributed a possible chapter at a time when the intent was to have fellow golfers do their own stories. In numerous conversations with Alan he helped me hone this into a more focused story and I am exceptionally grateful for his kind leadership. Two writers from my Williamson County Library Critique group read the manuscript in draft and offered both critique and encouragement. Thank you, Judith Walter and Laurie Michaud Kay. In 2014 I offered a not-yet-ready-for-publication version as an entry in the Williamson County Library writer's competition. *Disarmed* did not win, nor should it have done so, but the feedback I received from the judges was incredibly helpful to the final ready-for-publication version.

In place of a so-called Christmas newsletter, for years I have sent to a small group of friends essays of adventures from the year just past or from a year long past. When I sent the essay written in the Judge writing class to friends in 2011, several of them responded with encouragement and even contributed a story or two from their experiences with John and his arm. To David and Betsy Folland, John and Janice Collett, and to David Meadows especially I extend my thanks for your friendship and support.

As I brought the manuscript to completion, I pondered where and if I might sell it so it could have wide distribution. Over the ten years I have been writing, I have become disillusioned with the process of obtaining a place for my books in mainstream publication. There is incredible competition for an agent and then even more competition for such agent to sell a book, even one with the wide appeal I hope this one will have. In the best of all scenarios it may take two or three years to bring a book to the marketplace under these conditions. I don't have that long. John and I are in our 70's and we don't know how much longer we have together. More importantly, technology relative to amputees is changing at such a rapid pace that events I wrote about in 2011 and 2012 are already outdated.

With this background, I reached out to Mary Catharine Nelson, proprietor of Tennessee-based Ideas into Books, formerly Published by Westview, an independent publisher for print-on-demand books. I have worked with Mary Catharine on my two previous books, *Gotcha Covered: A Legacy of Service and Protection* and *Assisted Loving: The Journey Through Sexuality and Aging*. She has always offered the highest level of professionalism and at the same time an amazing capacity for warmth and support, bringing not only her personality but also her overflow horse manure for my garden to perk me up on days when my spirits sagged. When I sent her the manuscript for *Disarmed* at the end of 2014, she read it and within a week (and without consulting me first) she turned the Word document into a formatted pdf ready to upload into a published product. Of course I agreed, but with the caveat of a few edits to be done, and within a few weeks the first editions were printed. She is an amazing woman and I treasure her friendship and leadership.

In the outer circle of support are all the golfers, skiers, tennis players, church-goers, friends, PV vacationers, and anyone else who has interacted with John and me around his state of disarmament. Nearly every engagement with John involves a potential engagement with the arm and while occasionally people are afraid or disgusted with being in its presence, that experience is rare. More typically people are curious and then dismissive of it and or they just choose to join in with accepting the inevitable of having a threesome of themselves, John, and that damn artificial arm. And that's where the smiles begin.

About the Author

Ginger Manley did not discover she wanted to be a writer until she was in her fifties. Before that she was a registered nurse and advance practice nurse, a certified sex therapist, a wife, mother, and almost completely normal person. Once she was taken under the spell of writing she has not been able to stop telling stories, inspired by a collection of vintage aprons she inherited, the antics of her grandchildren and other family members, the questions asked about sexuality by her students and readers, and now the lifelong story of her relationship with her husband, John, and his artificial arm.

When she is not writing, she works part-time at Vanderbilt University Medical School, teaching whoever will listen about sexuality, health care, and ethical practices for today's doctors and nurses. In her free time, she is an avid gardener of her one-acre home place in Franklin, TN, where she composts anything that is biodegradable. She plays an occasionally decent round of golf but mostly sees the game as a vehicle for friendly associations with buddies in beautiful settings followed by food and drink. She, John, and the arm travel widely when given the opportunity to do so and are looking forward to whatever life journeys await them in the last couple decades of their lives.

Her newest book, *Proud Flesh*, a rollicking novel of sex, God, and dancing and the mother issues that wrap around each of these topics, will be released later in 2015.

Ginger can be reached at ginger@gingermanley.com

CPSIA information can be obtained at www.ICGtesting.com
Printed in the USA
BVOW08s1413060515

399277BV00001B/64/P